Weird Wild Wonderful Mandalas
Nontraditional Unique Mandalas

by Jennie Hennesay
Copyright 2016

This book is dedicated to my five wonderful children who, inspite of everything (or maybe because of it), blossomed into loving, caring, unique individuals each with their own talents, and in so doing taught me that it's OK to be yourself, whether it fits the "social norm" or not.

Too many people have guided me along this path to mention them all, but I'd like to give special thanks to Marilyn Southmayd for showing me how to get this book published.

Also special thanks to Becky Alexander Conrad for her encouragement, inspiration and guidance in my coloring and mandala making endeavor.

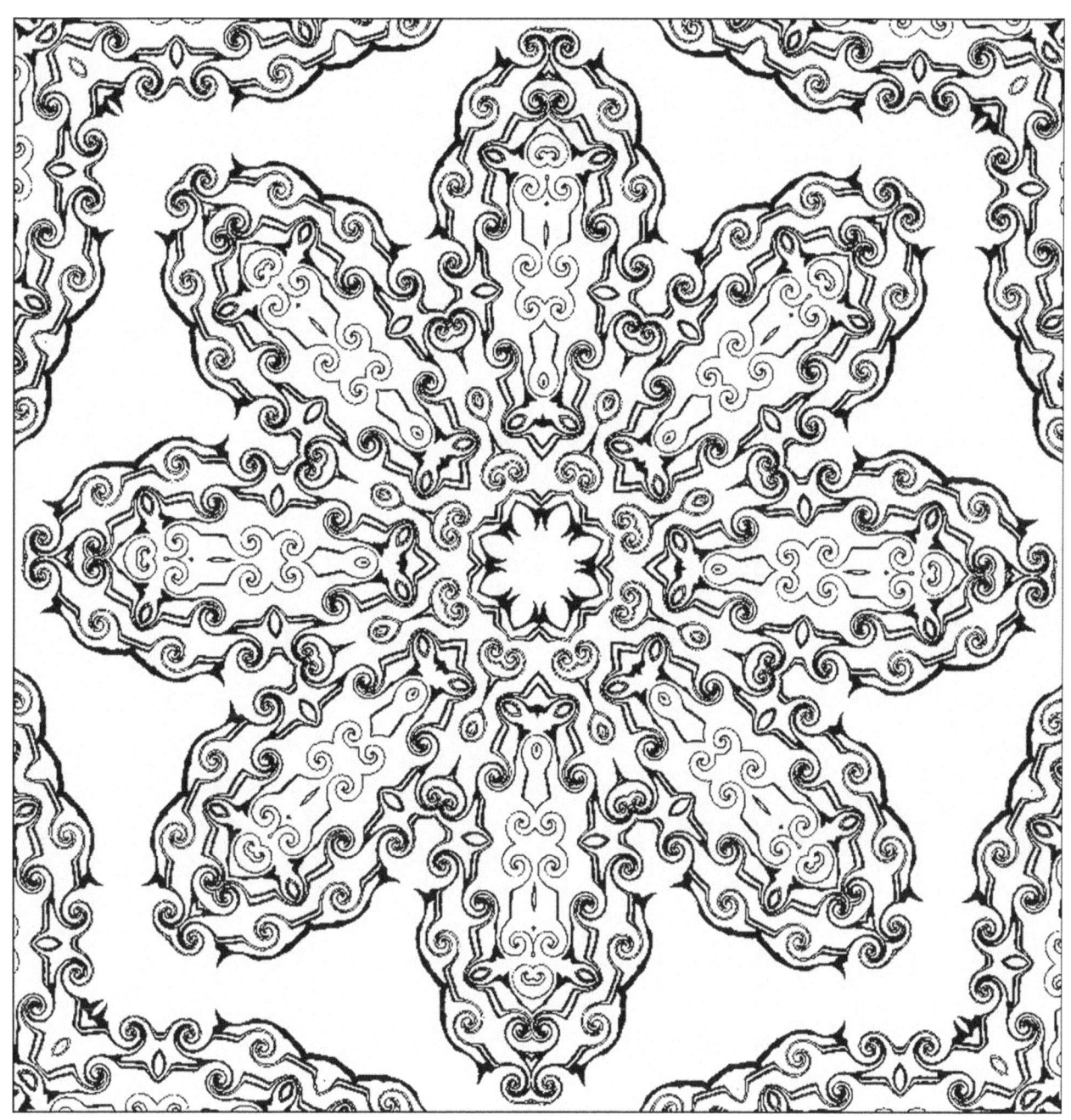

Bold Fantasy

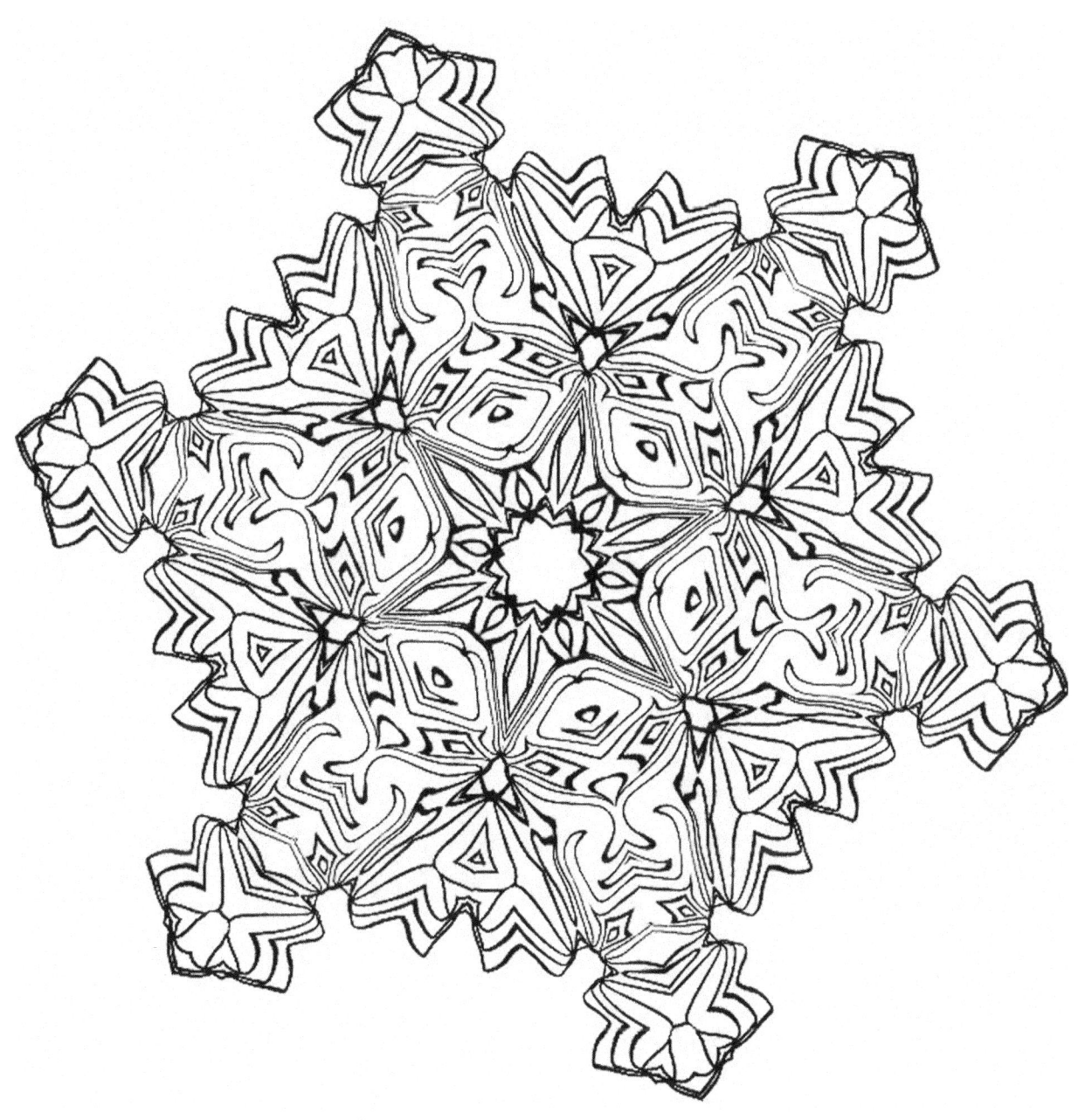

Cog

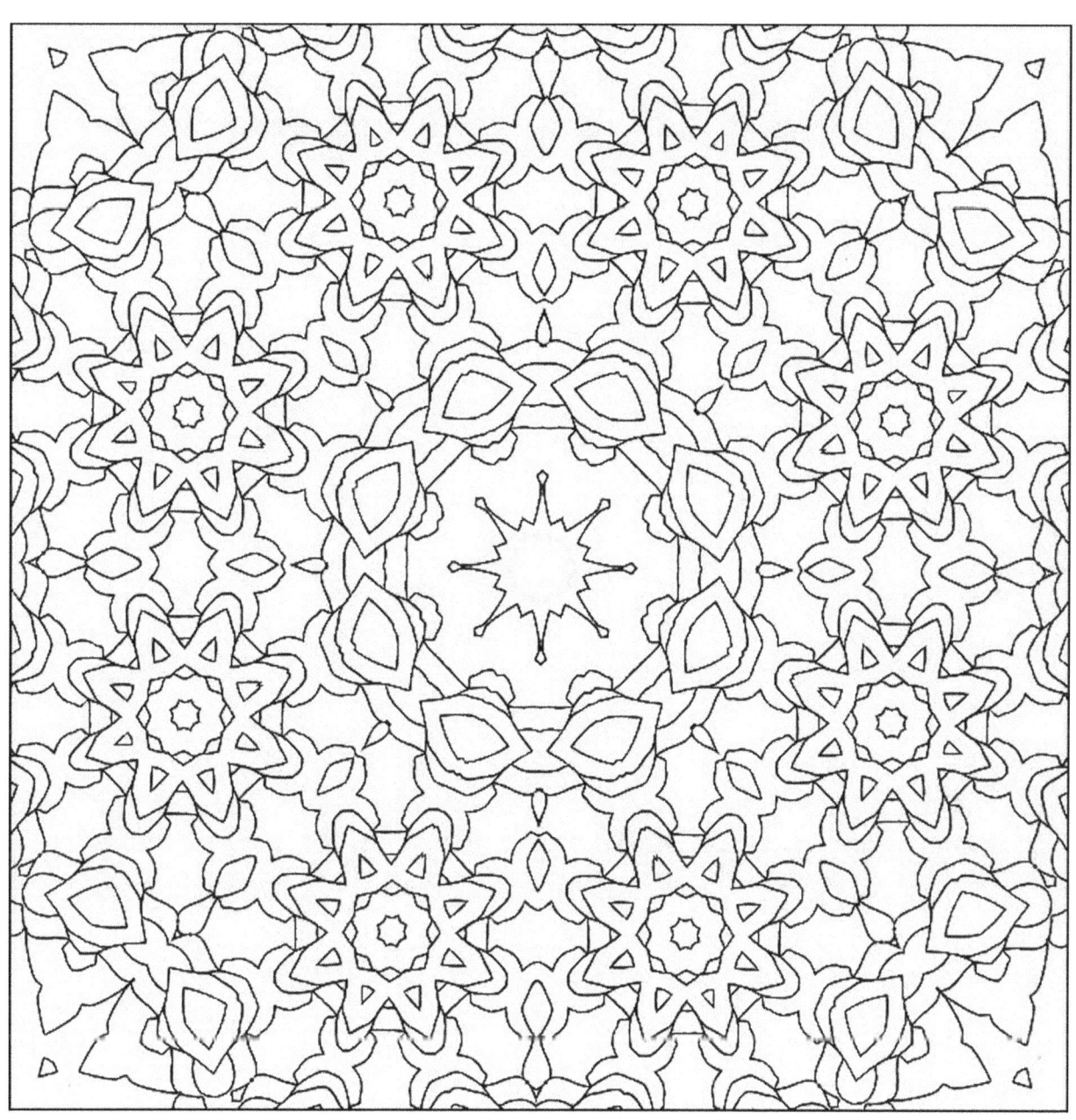

Daisy Mosaic

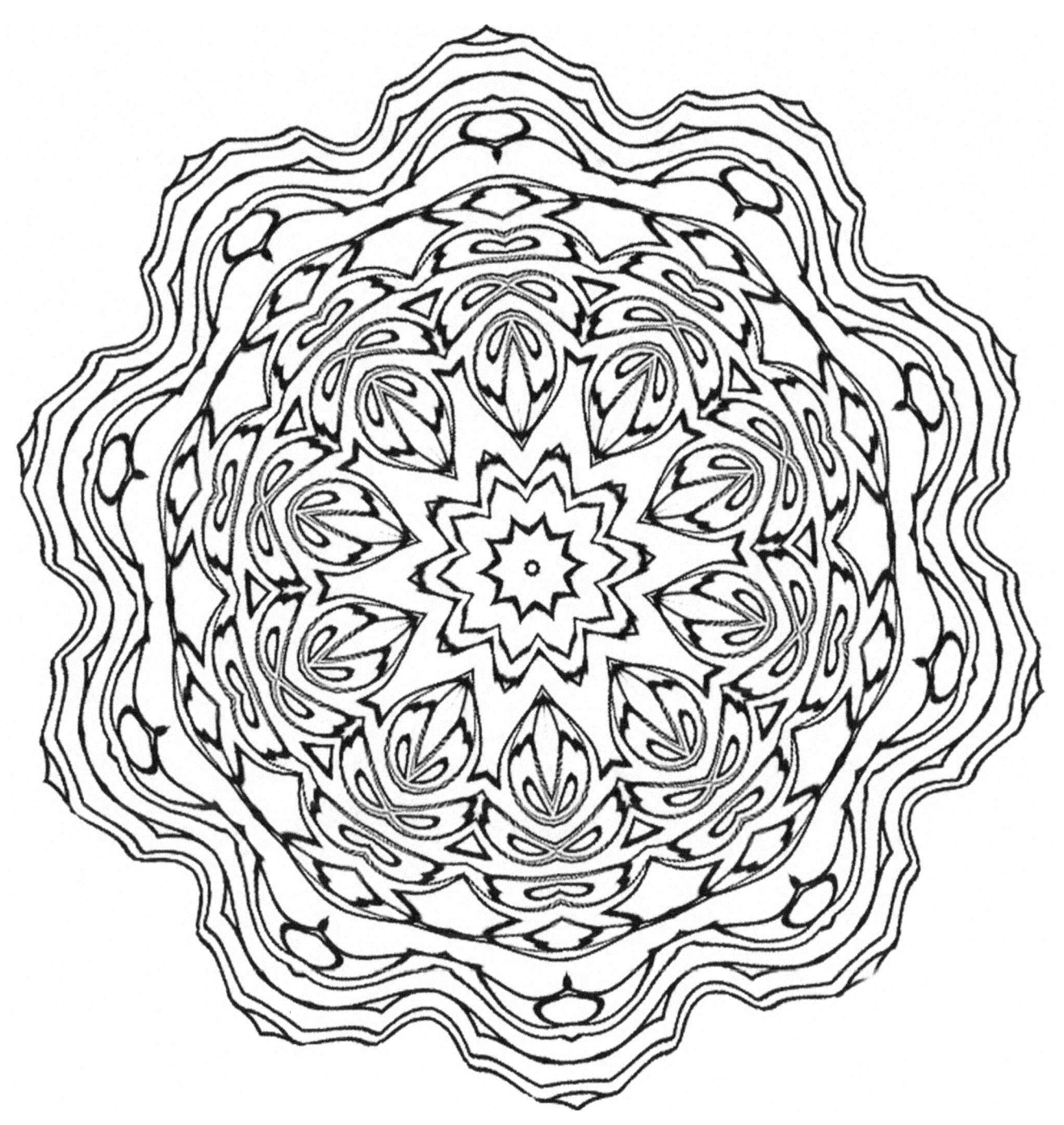

Fern

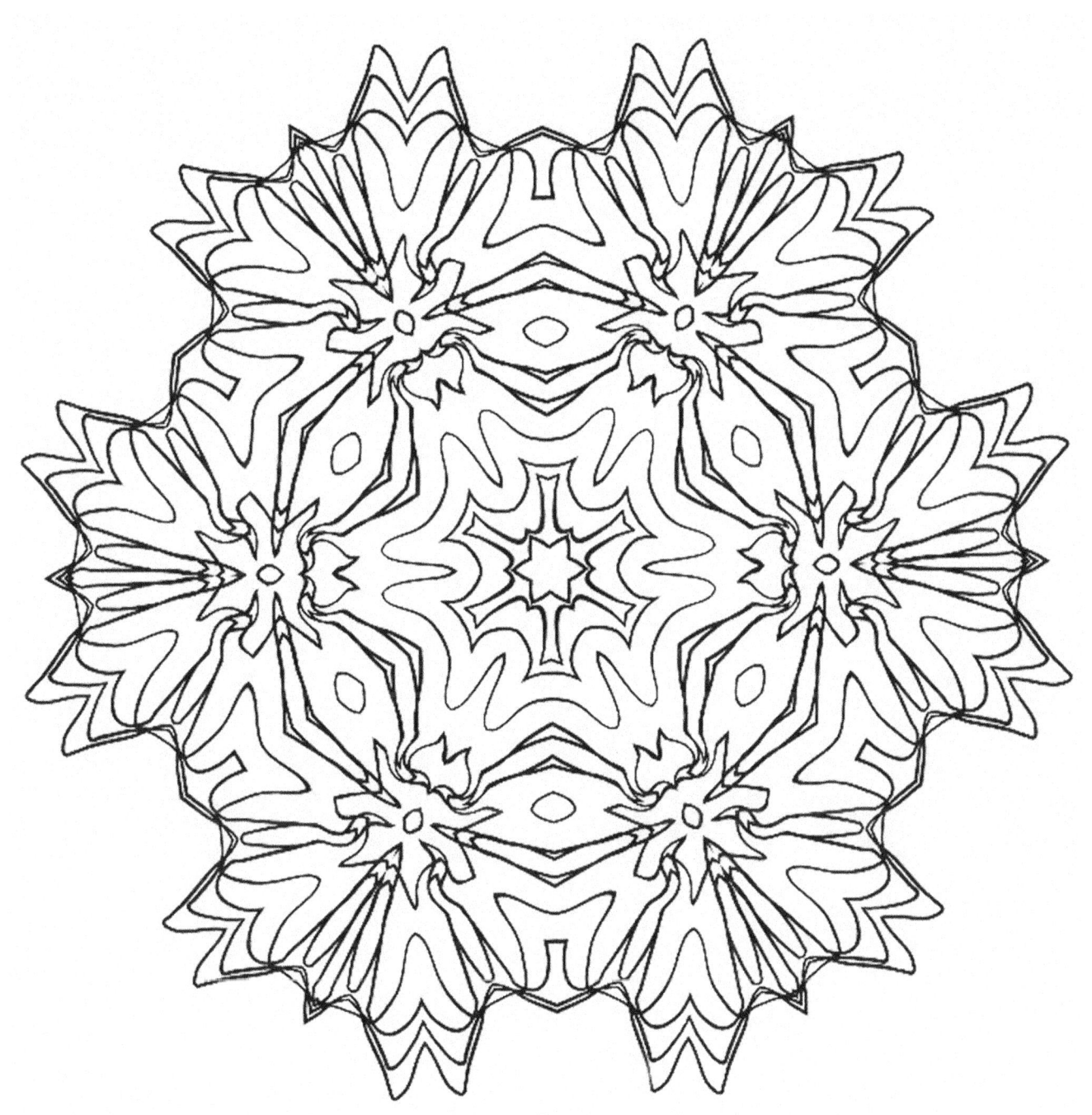

Gaea

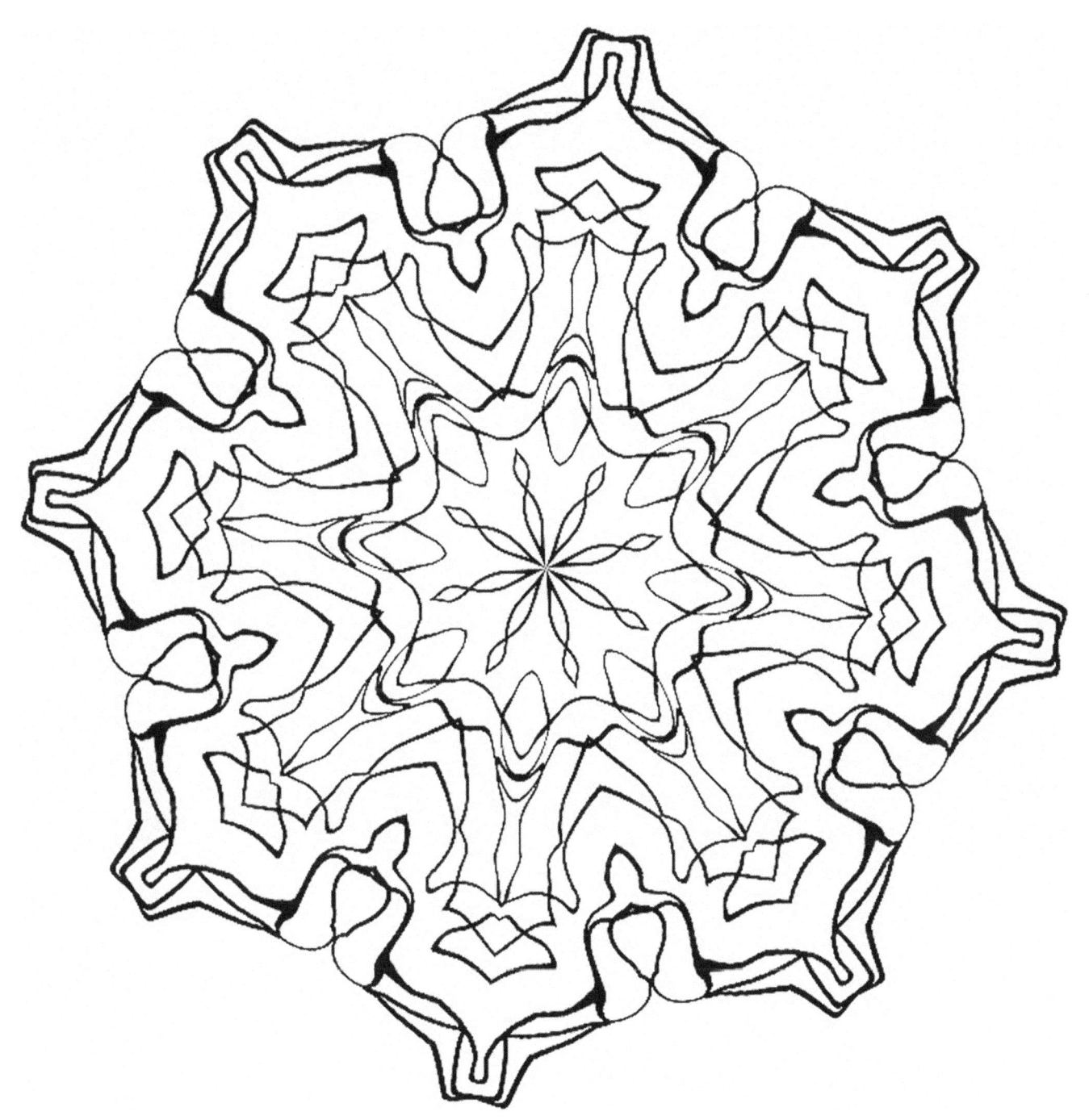

Latch

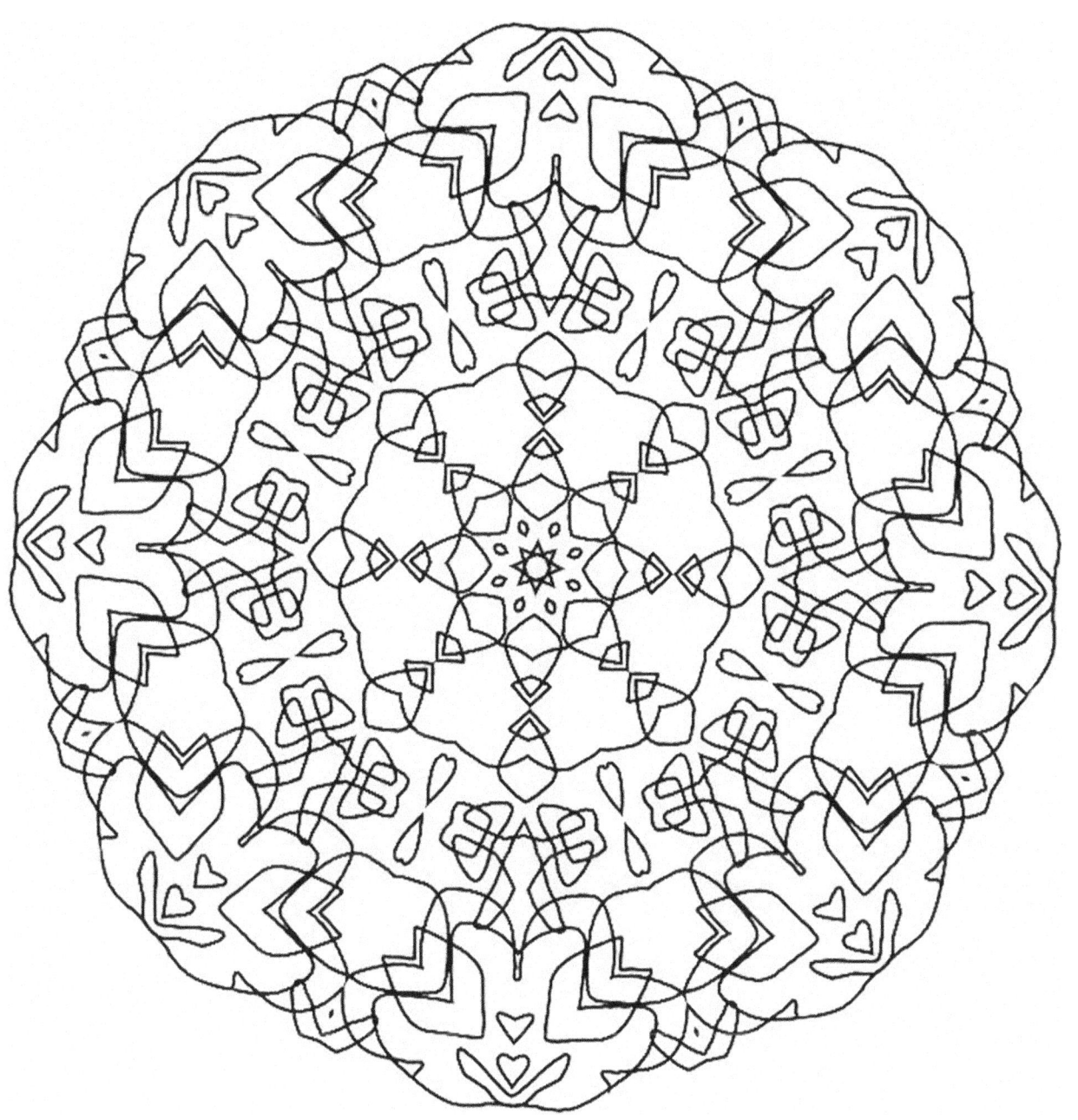

Leaf & Arrow Maze

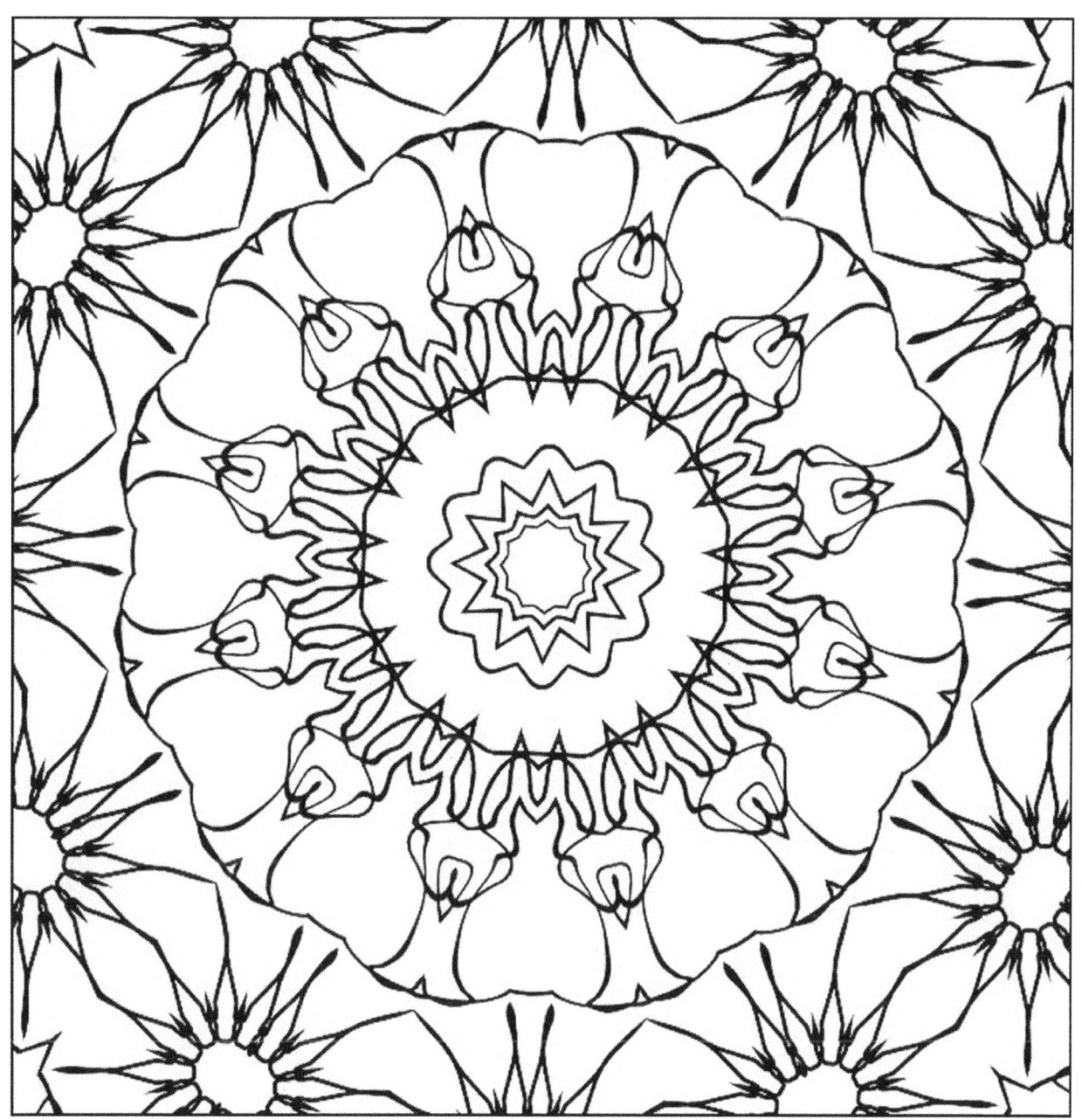

Lighted Columns

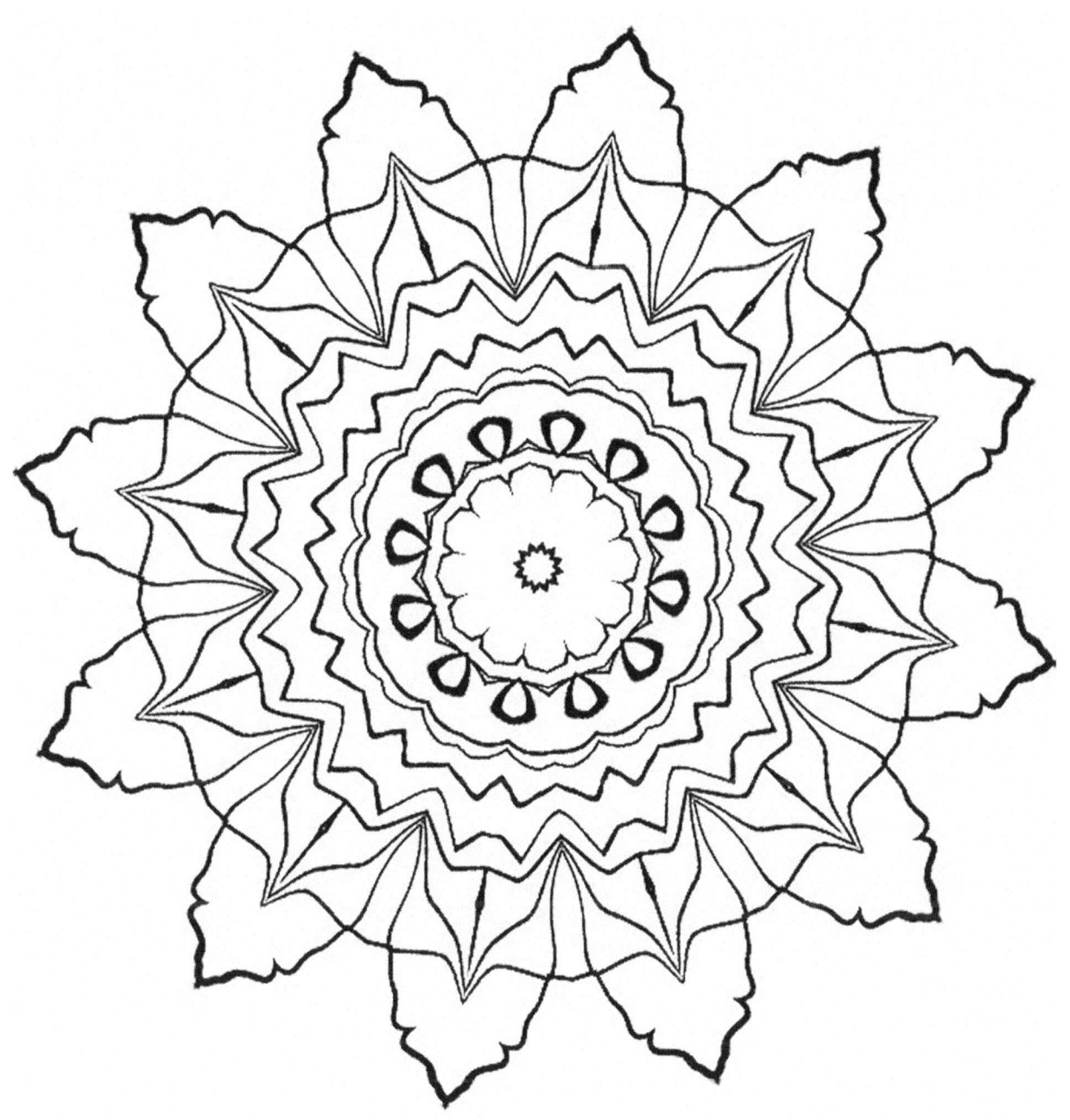

Oak

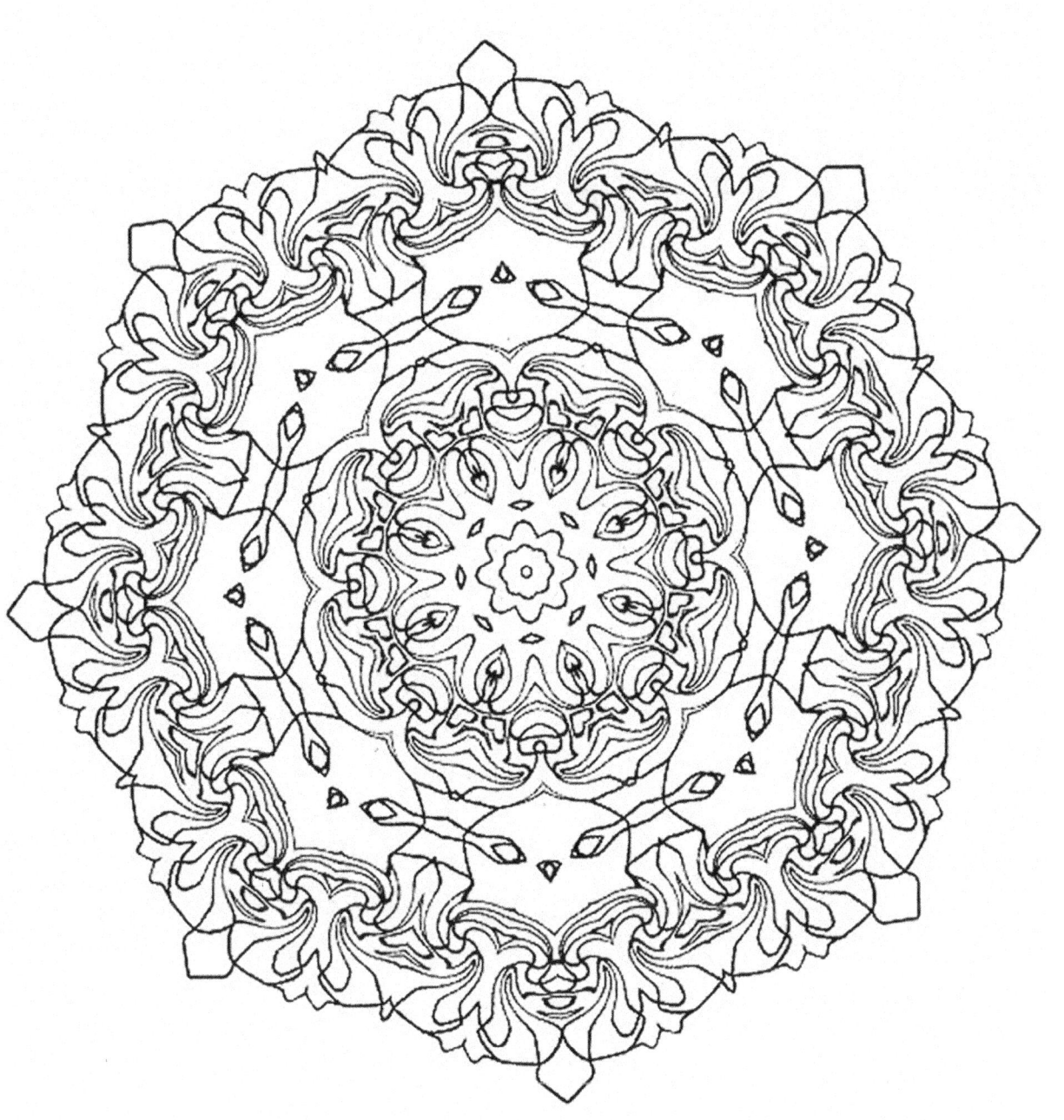

Opulence

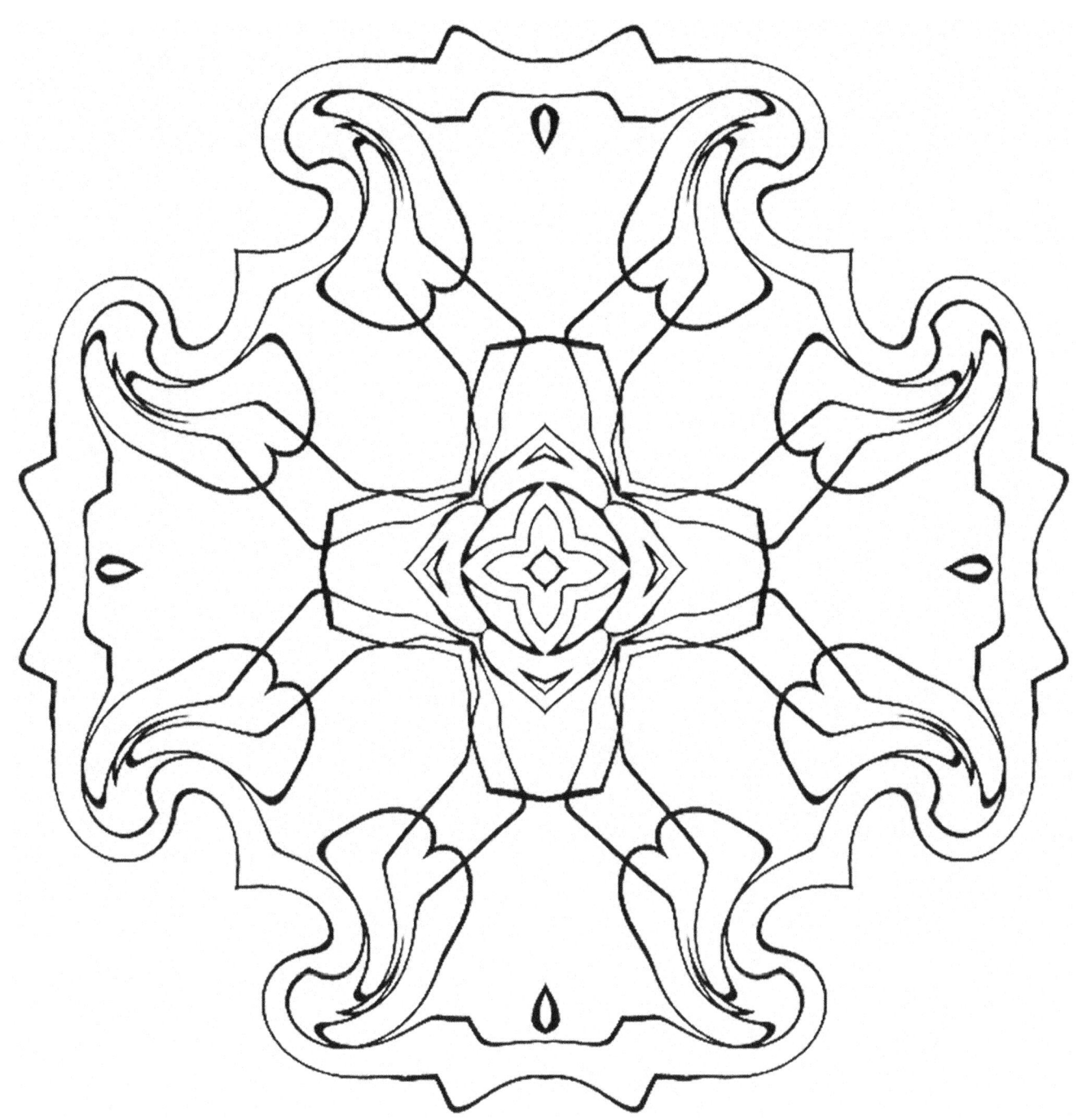

Ornate Cross

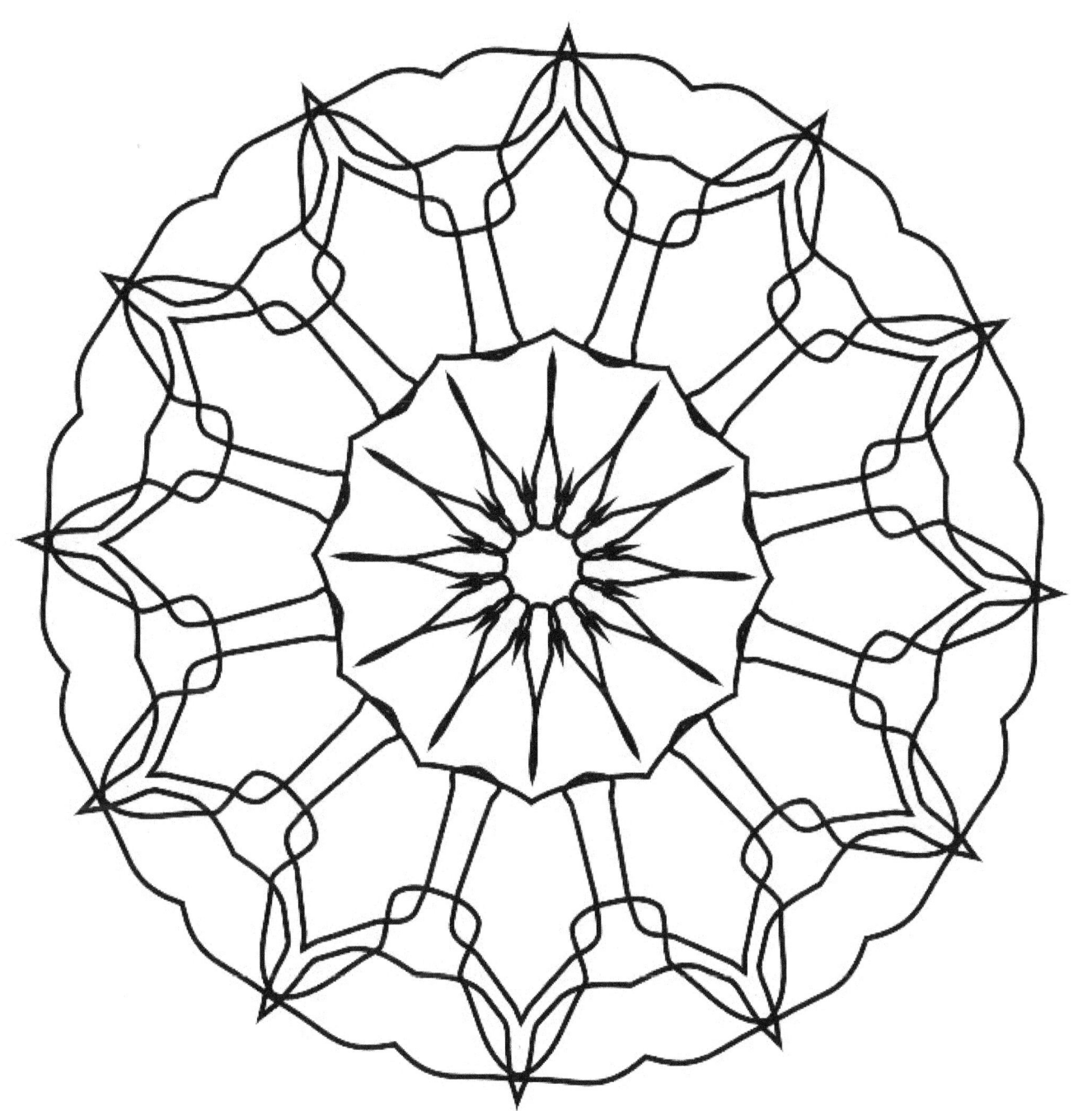

Peaked Columns

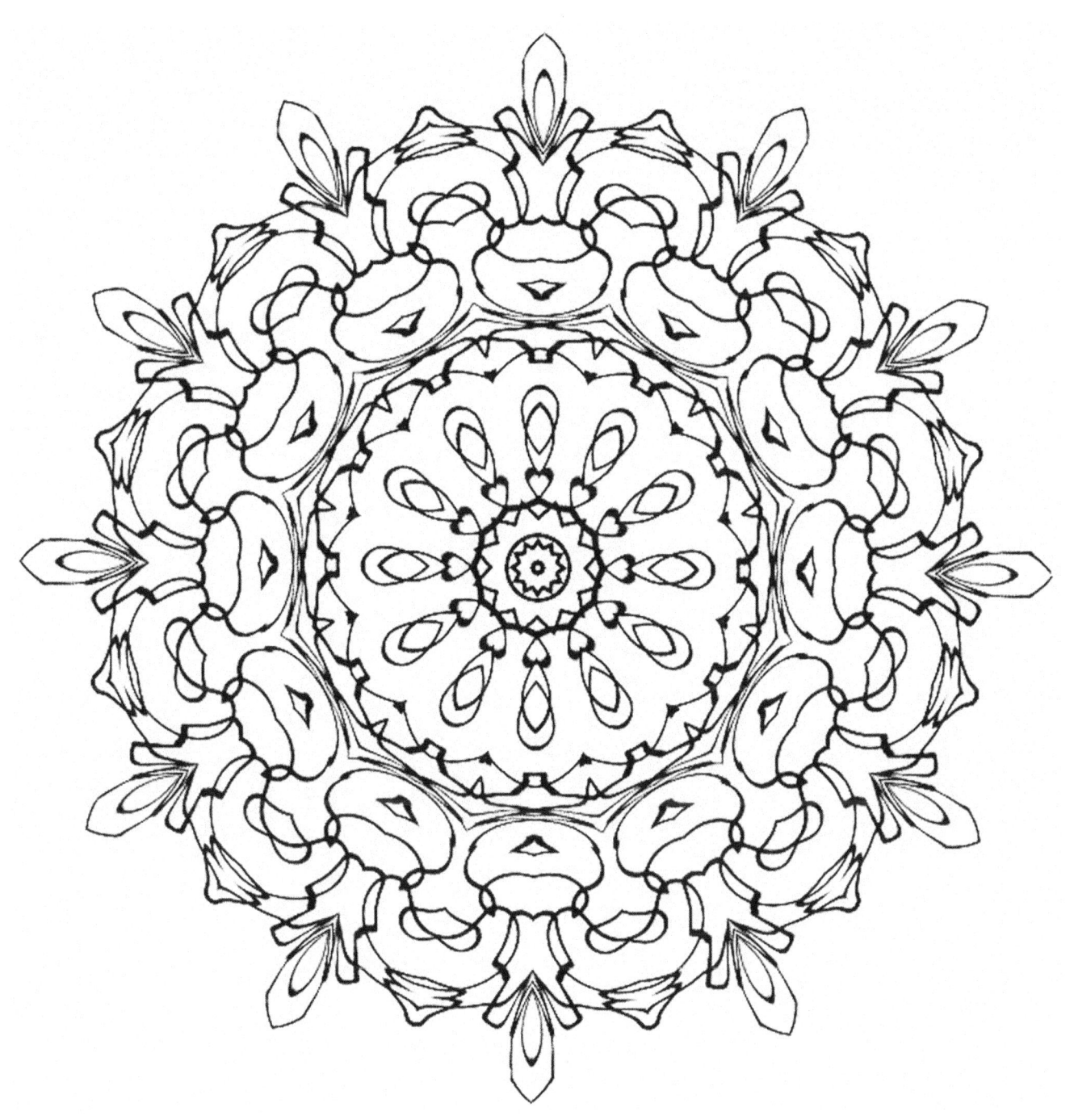

Potted Plants

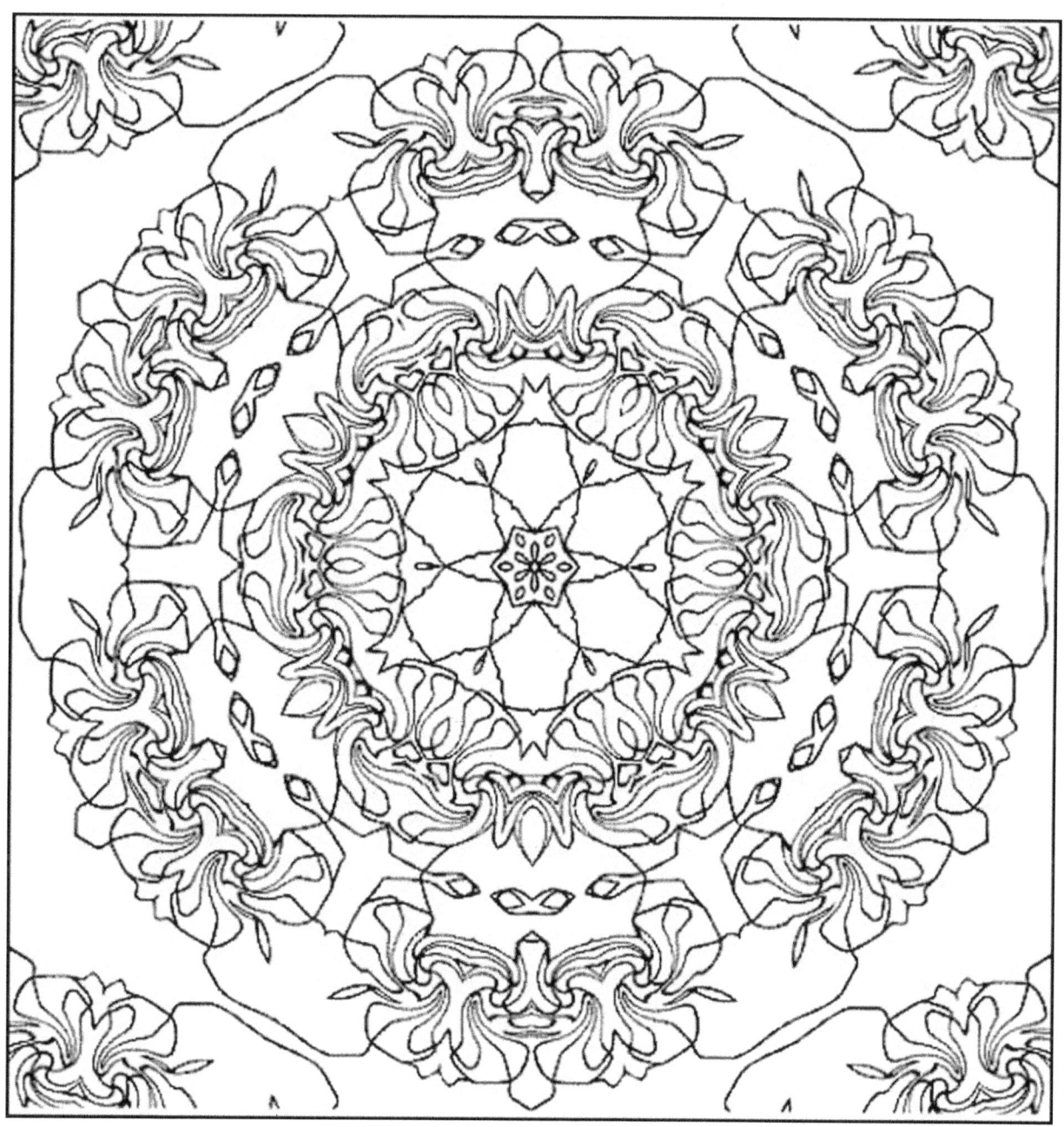

Pride

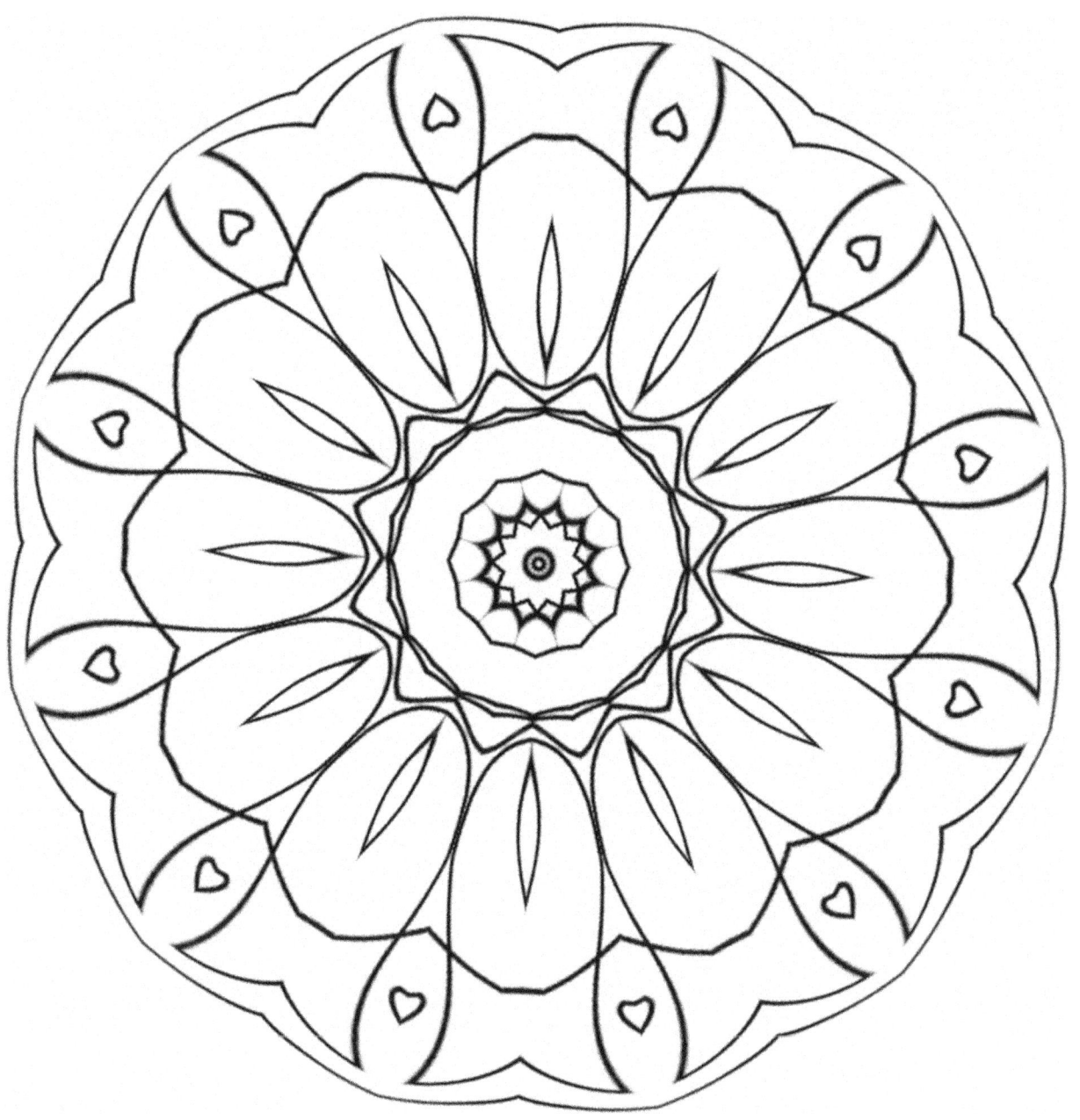

Puffed Star

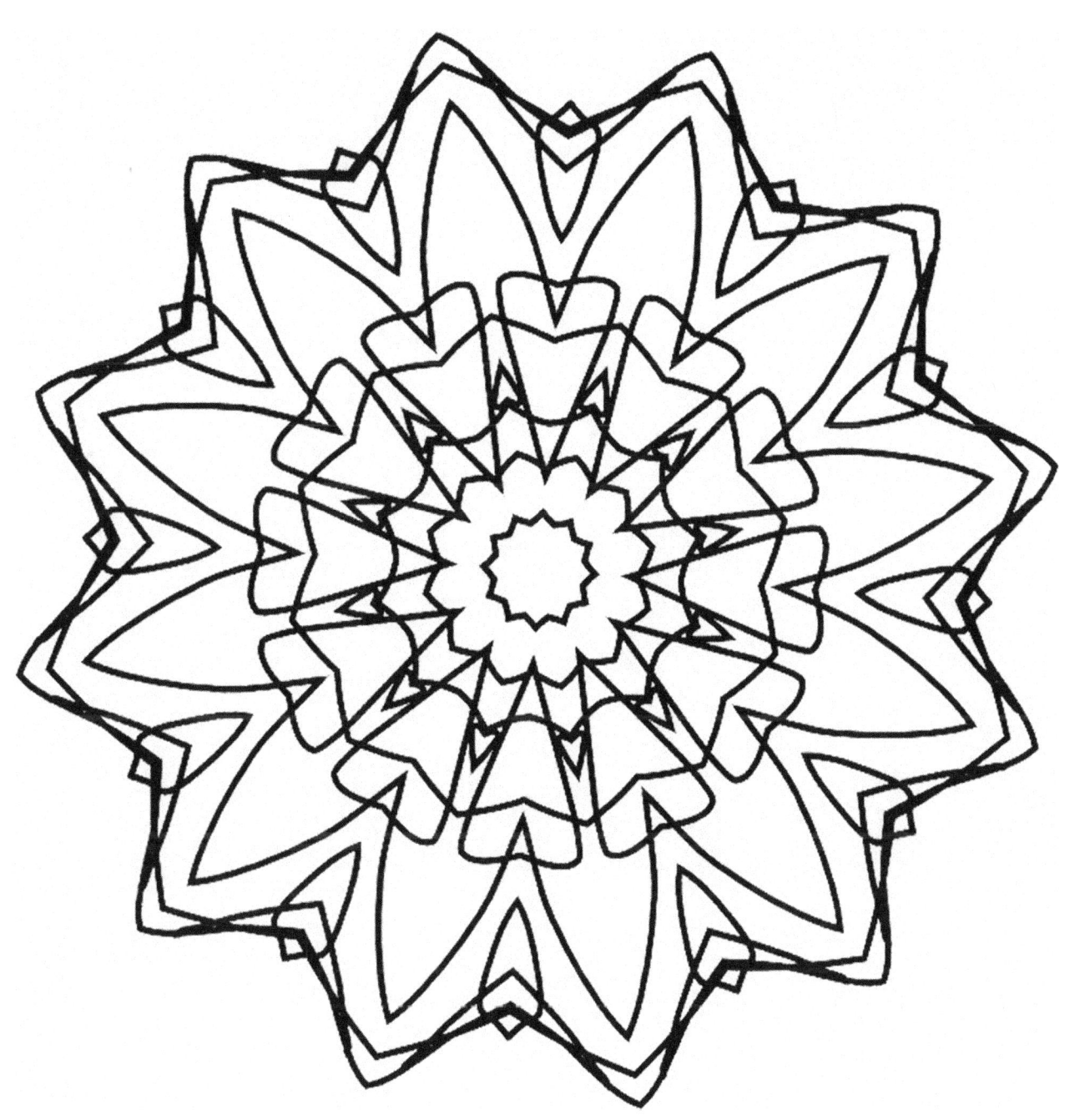

Refractions

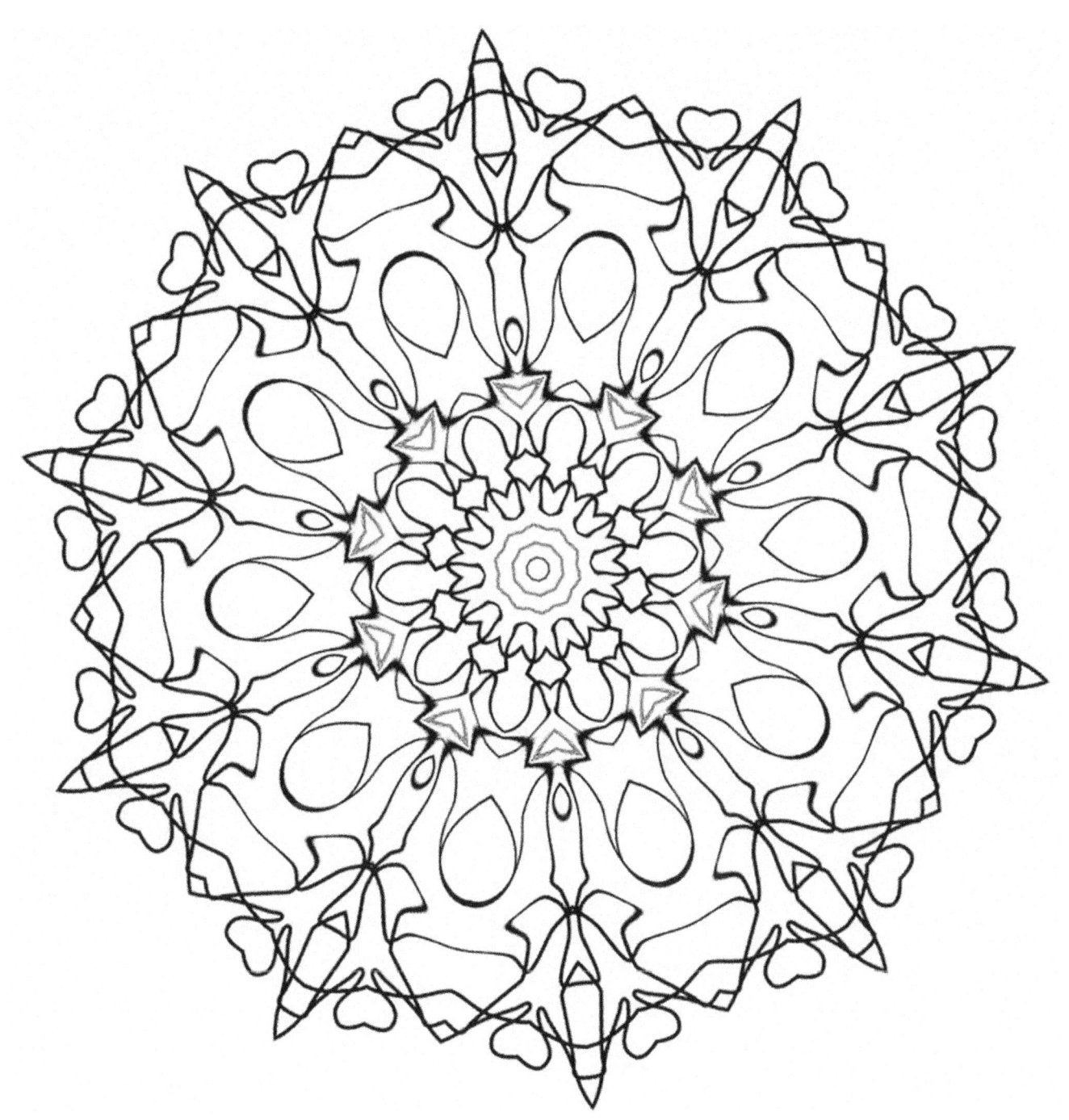

Rockets

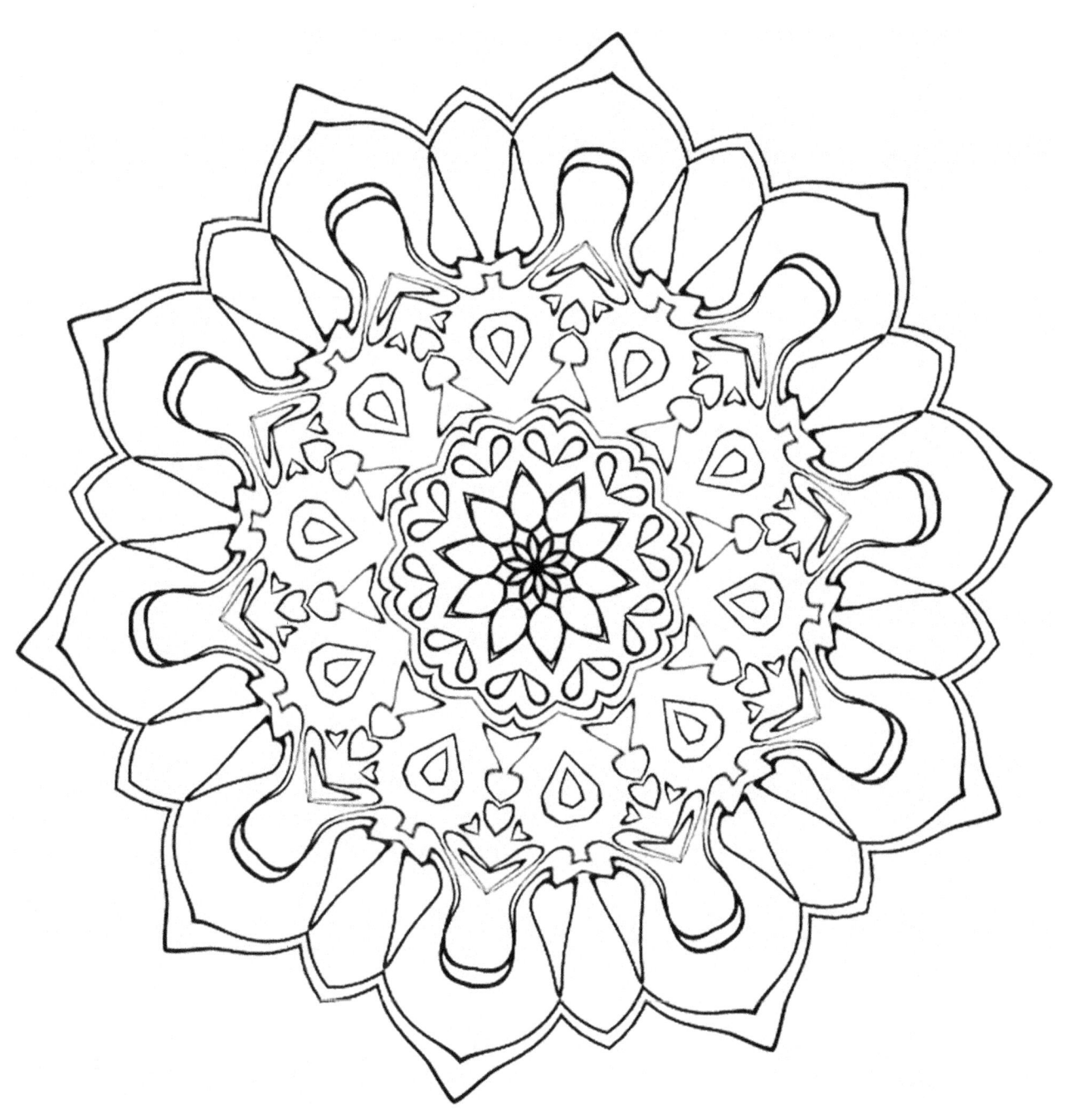

Shirred Pillow

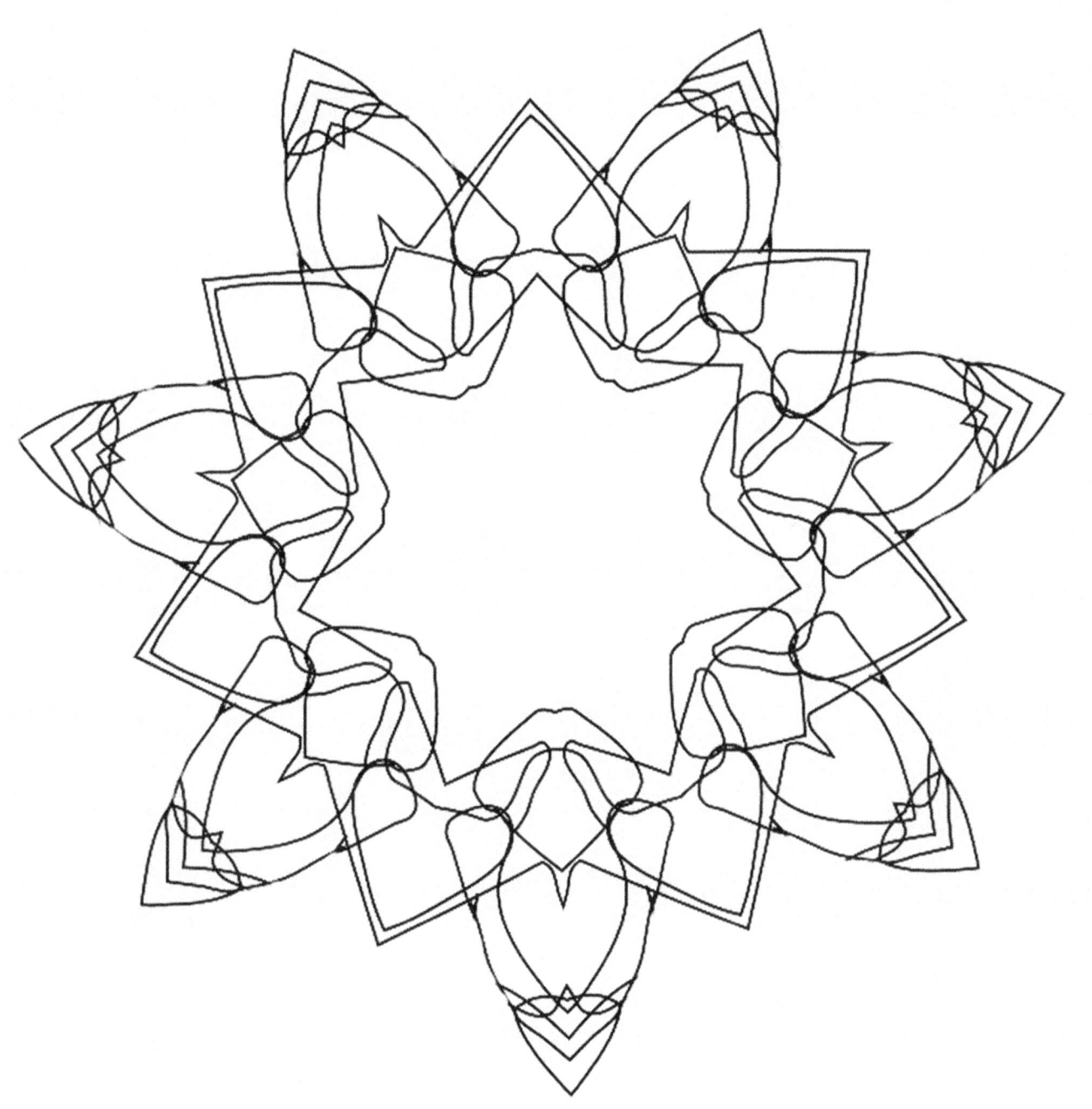

Shuriken

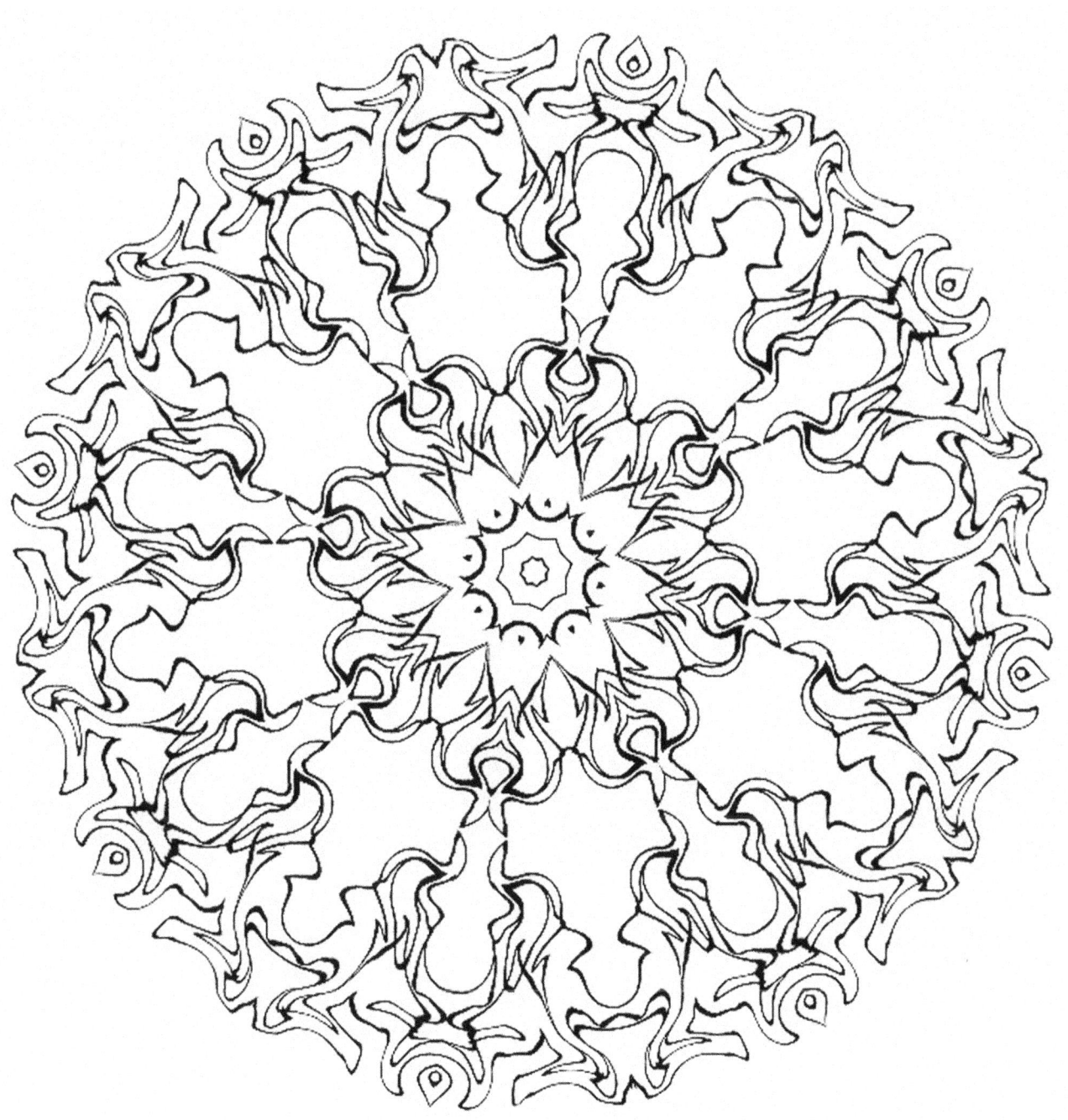

Silhouette

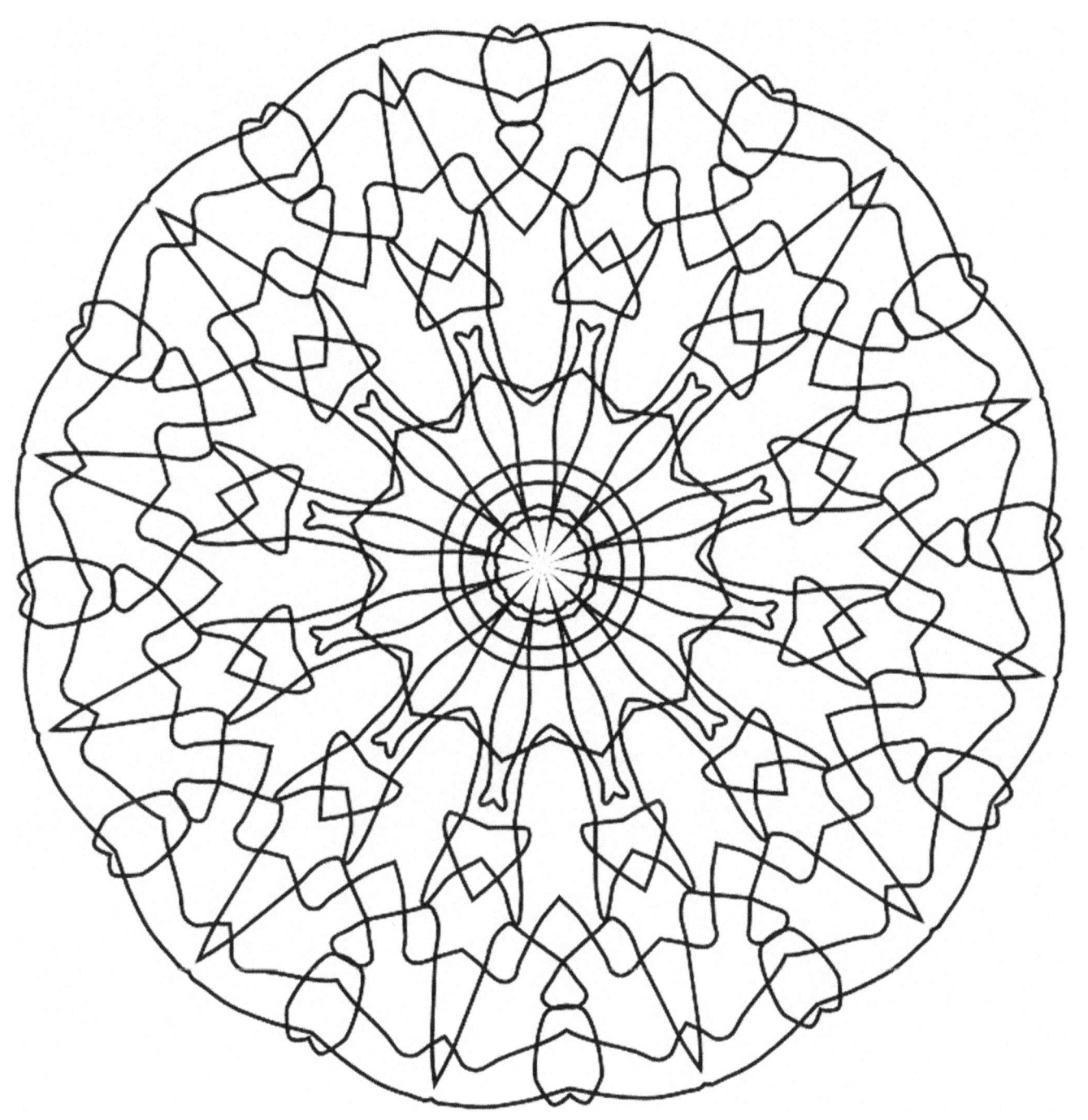

Spokes

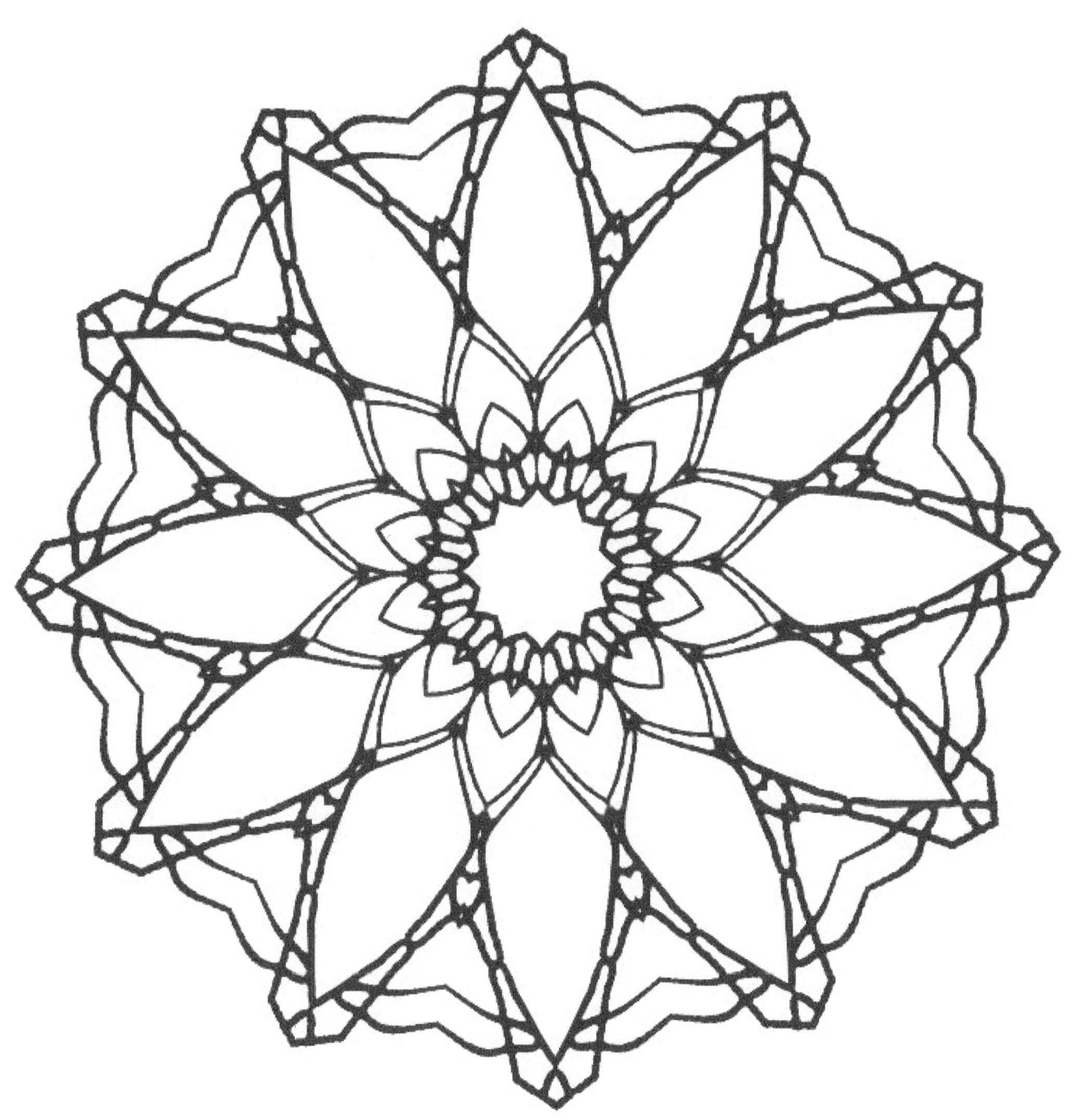

Stained Glass Flower

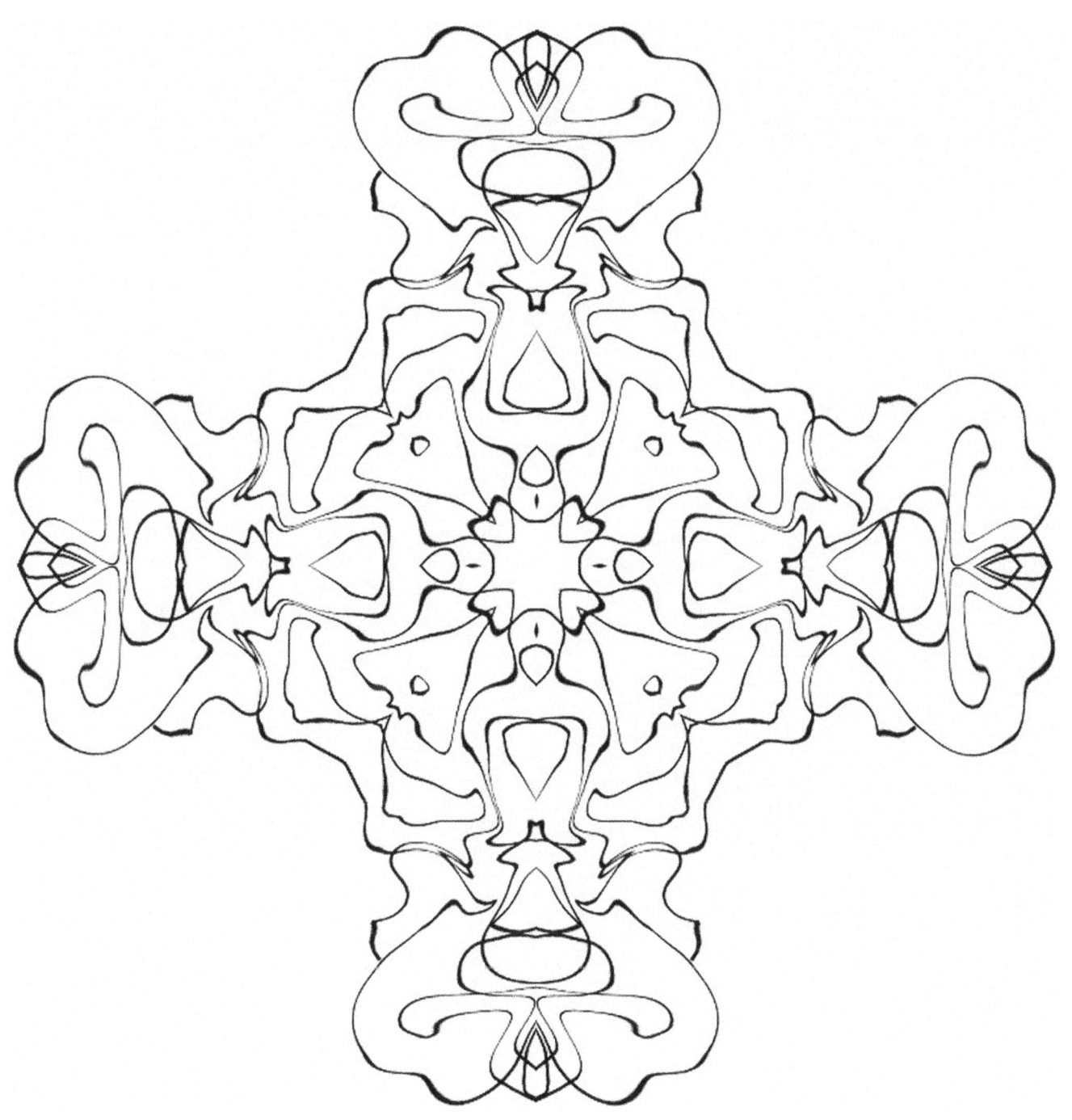

Steampunk Cross

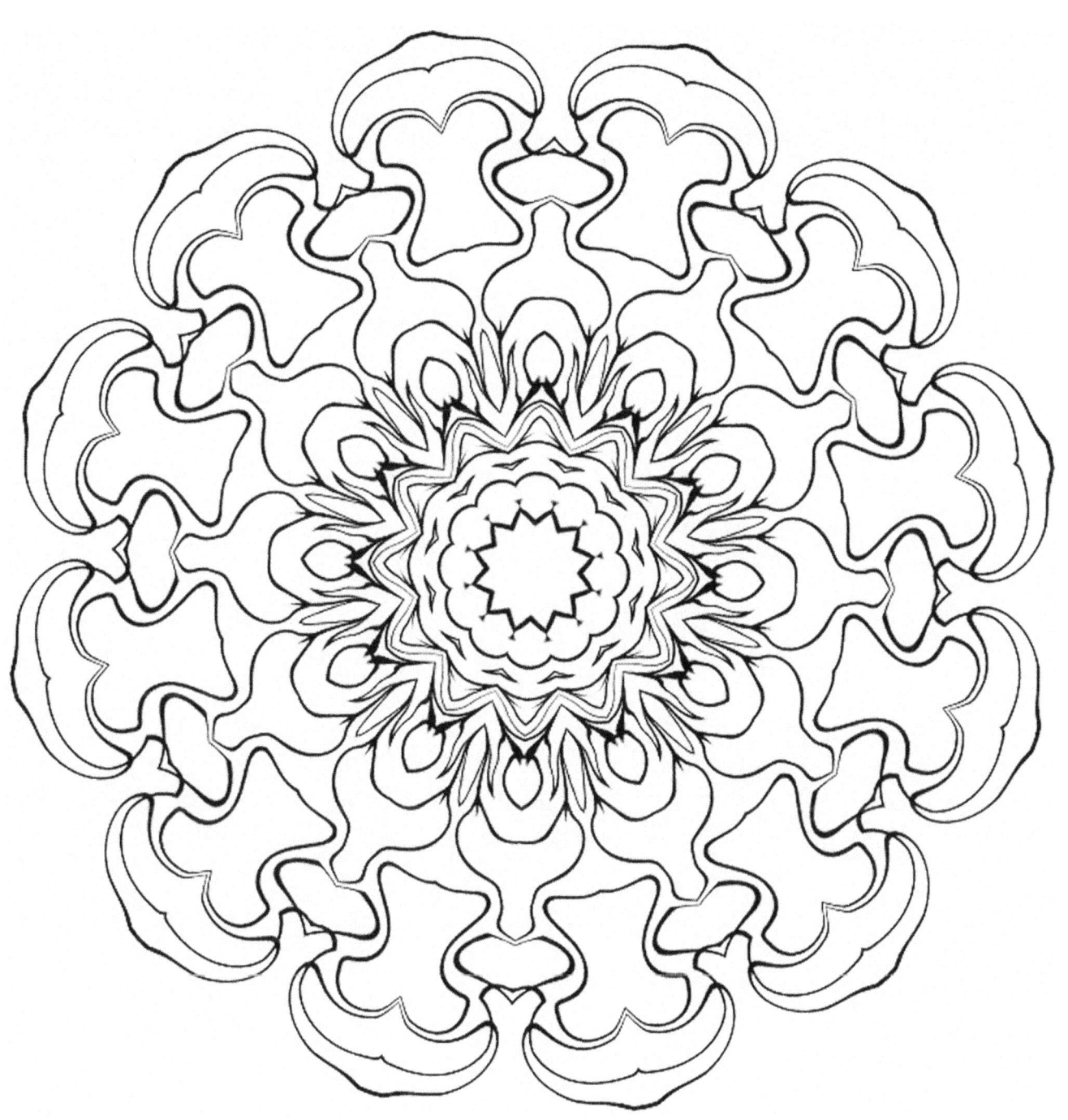

Storm

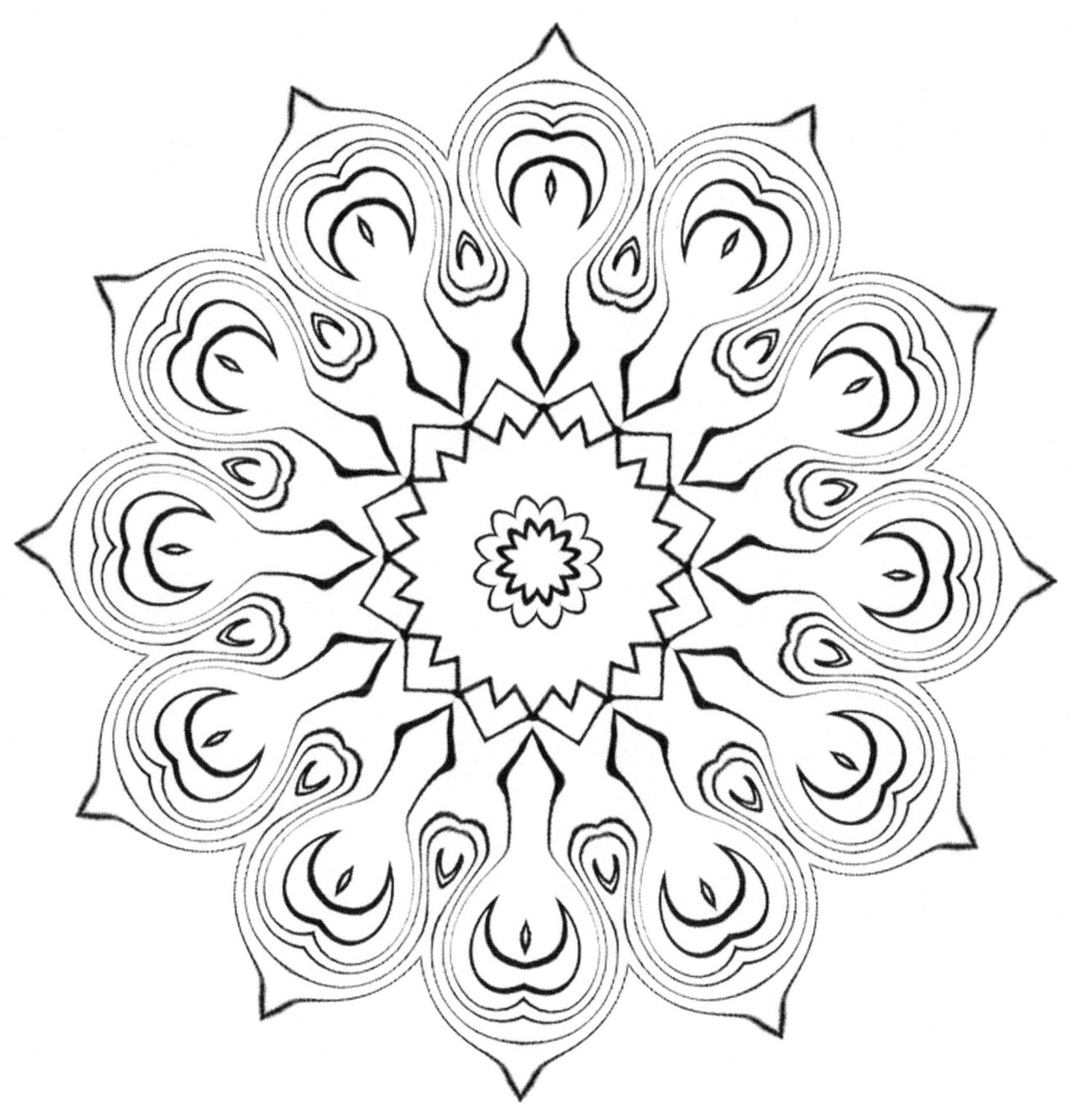

Sunshine & Showers

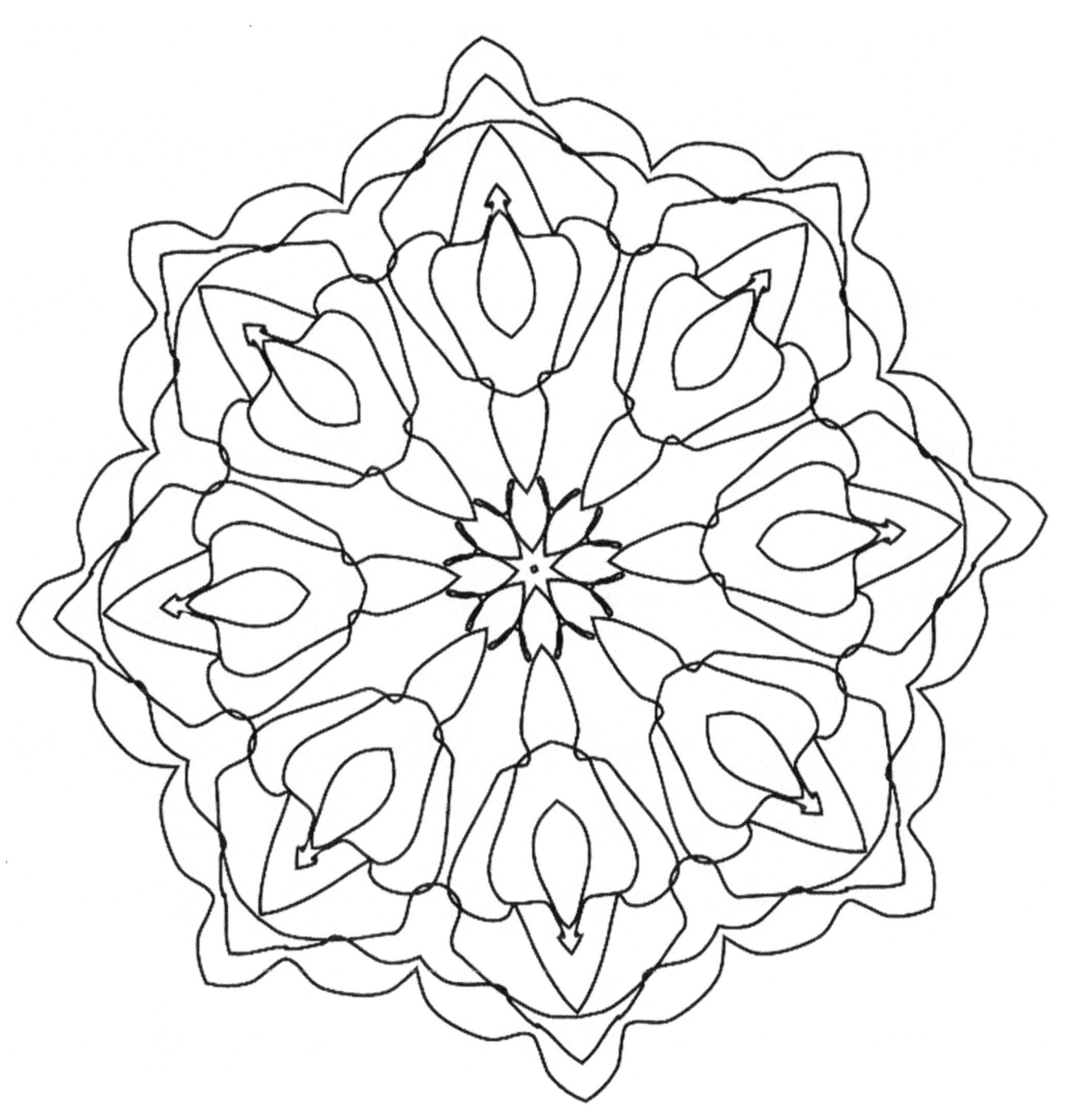

Symetry

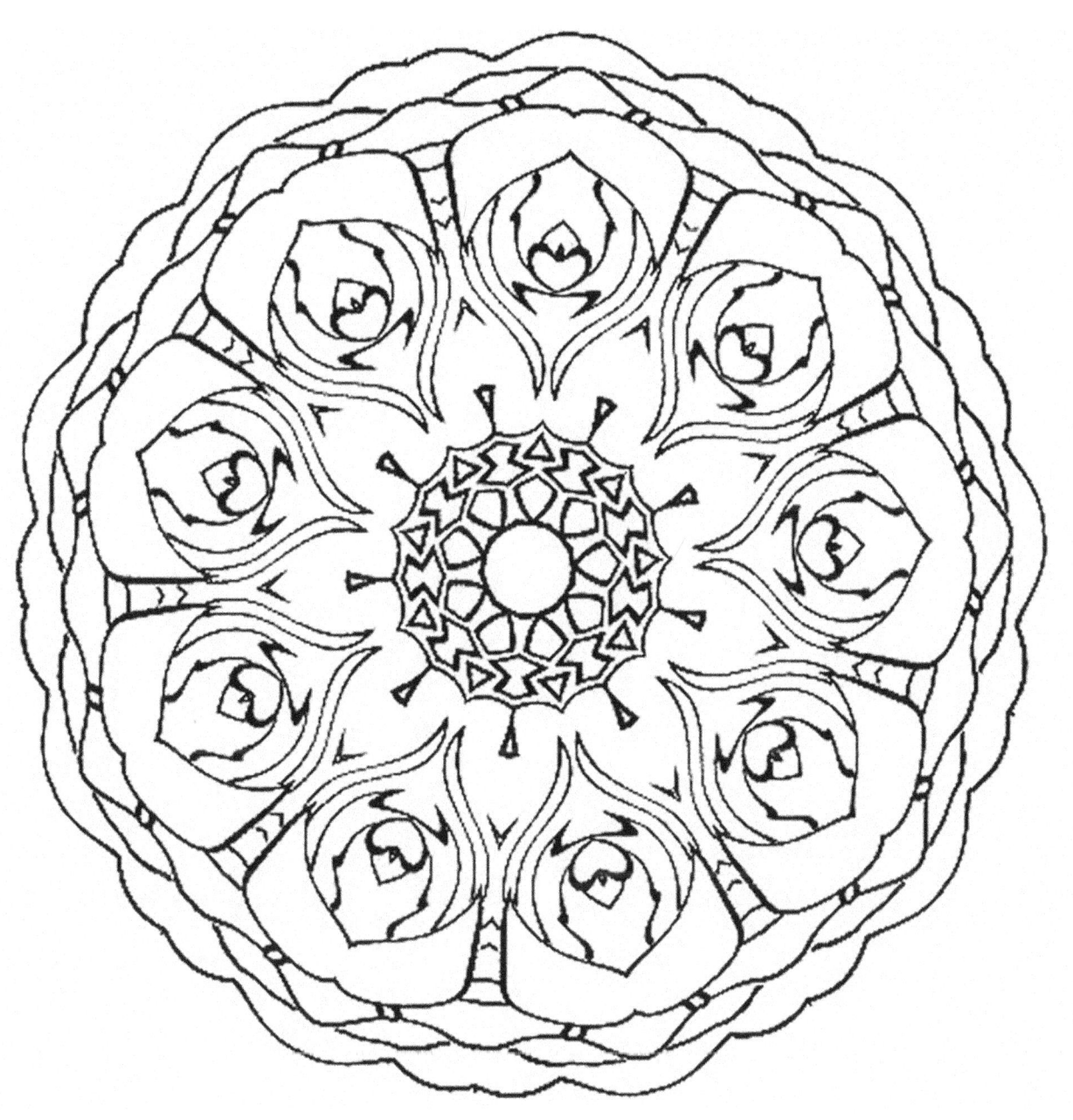

Tiki Torch

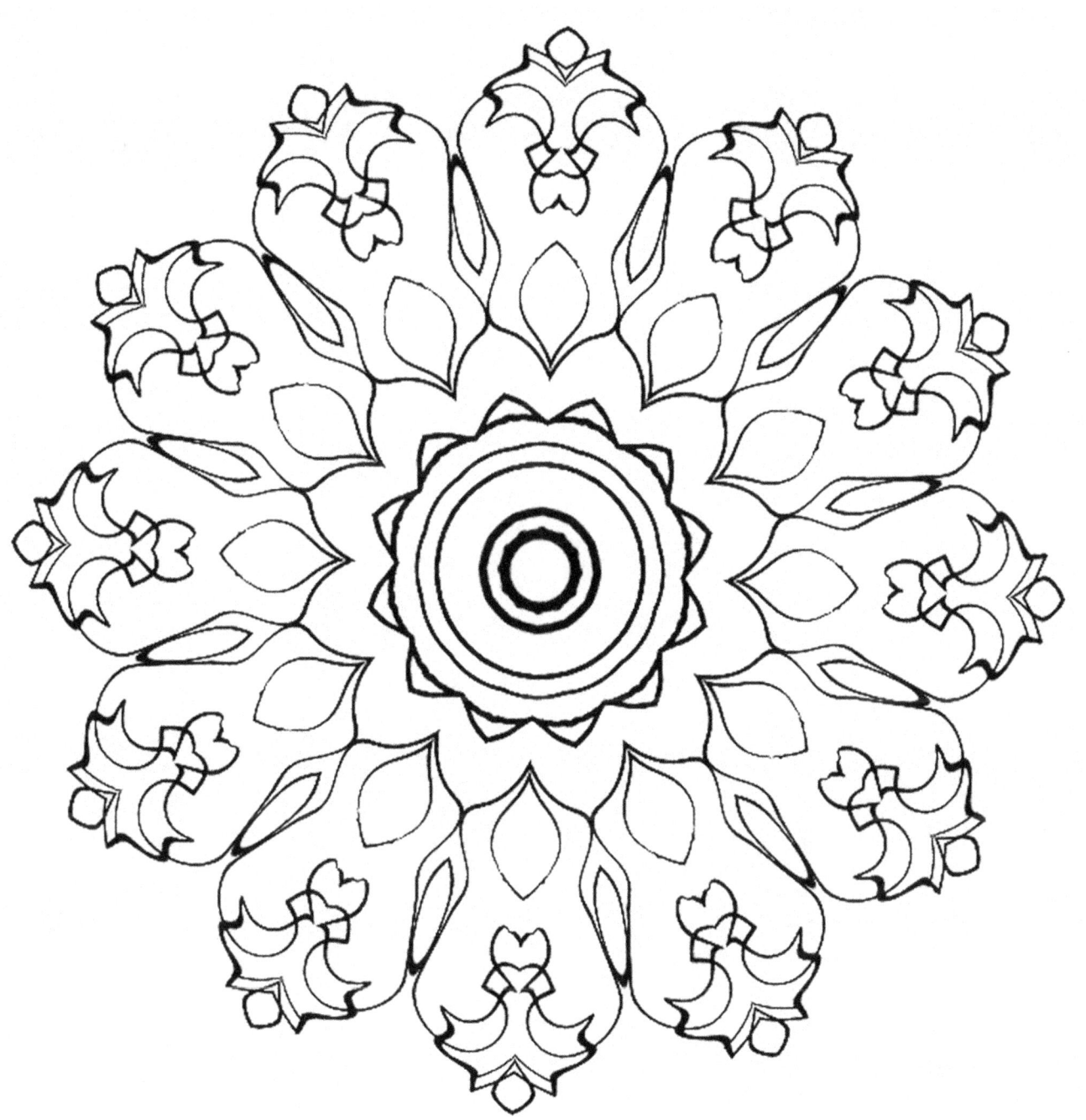

Topsy Turvy

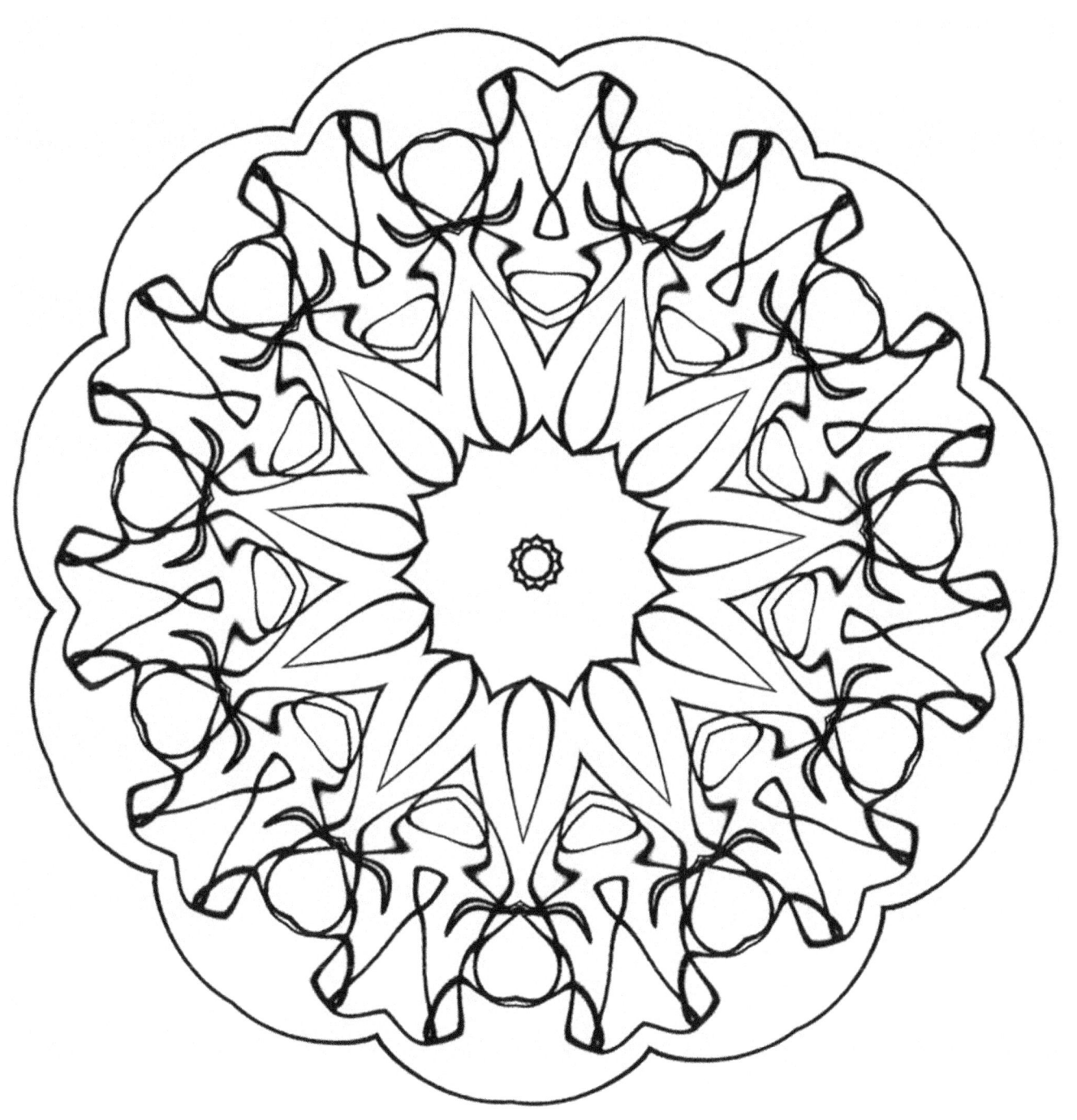

Tragedy

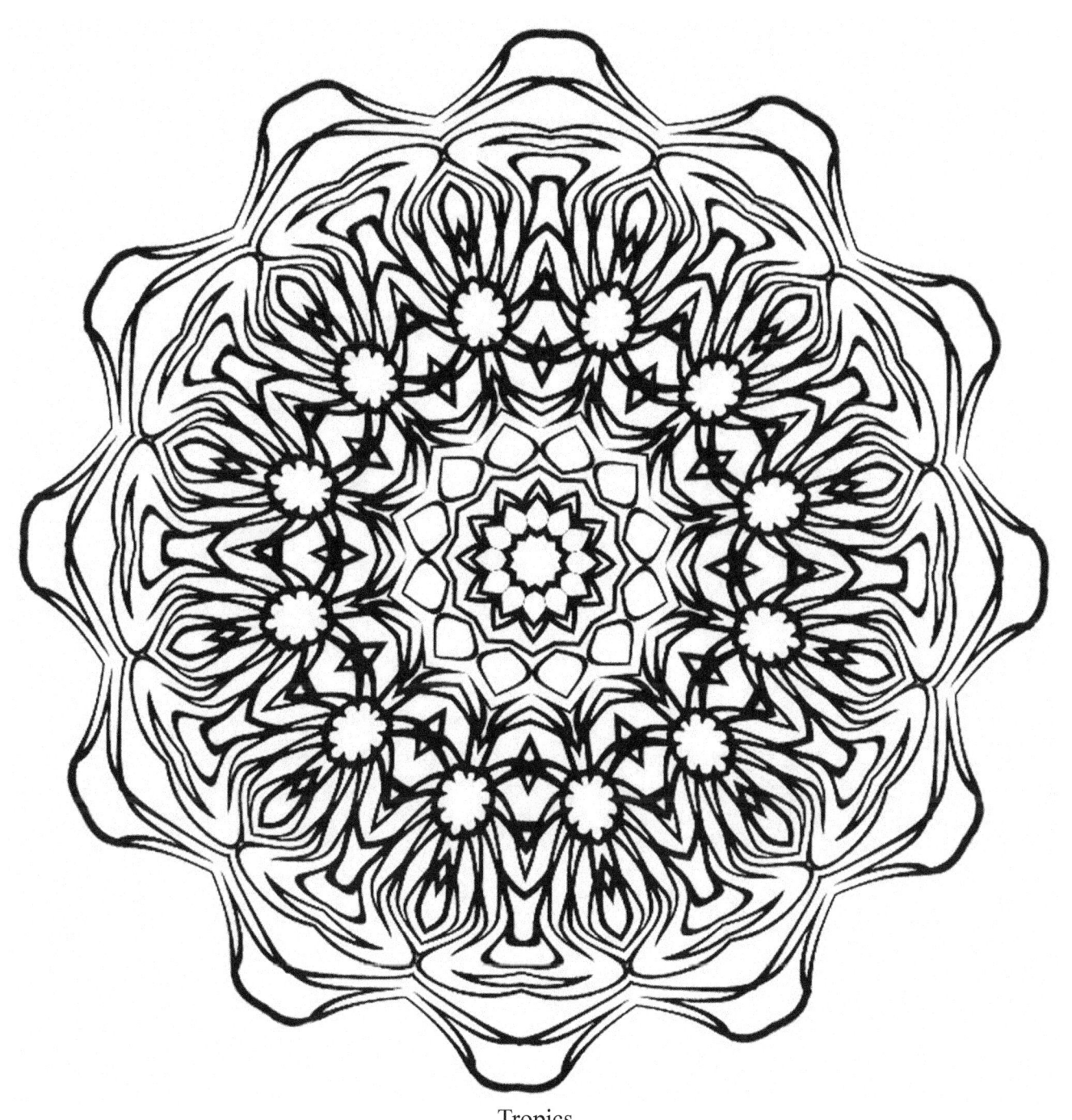

Tropics

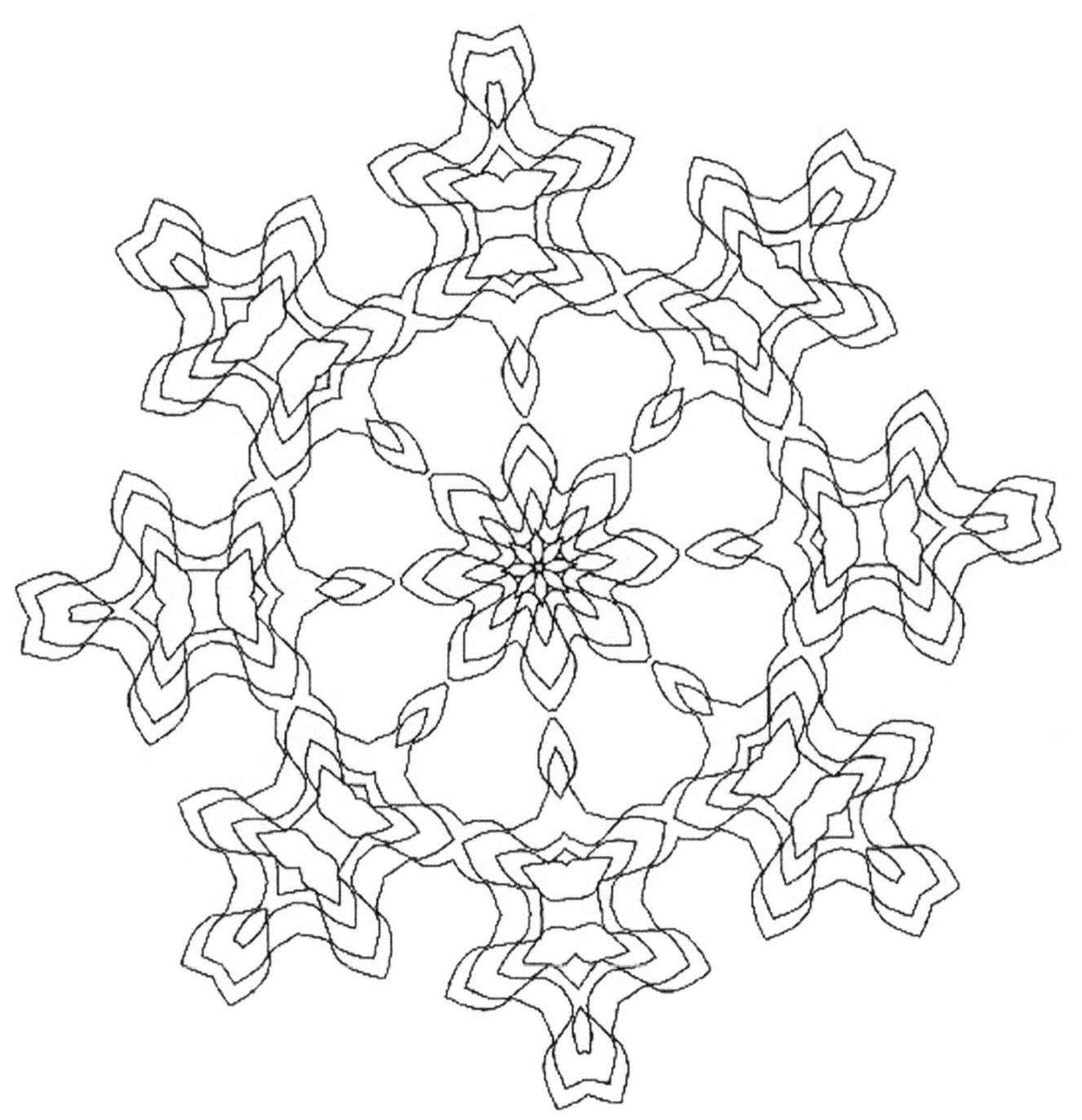

Twist & Turn

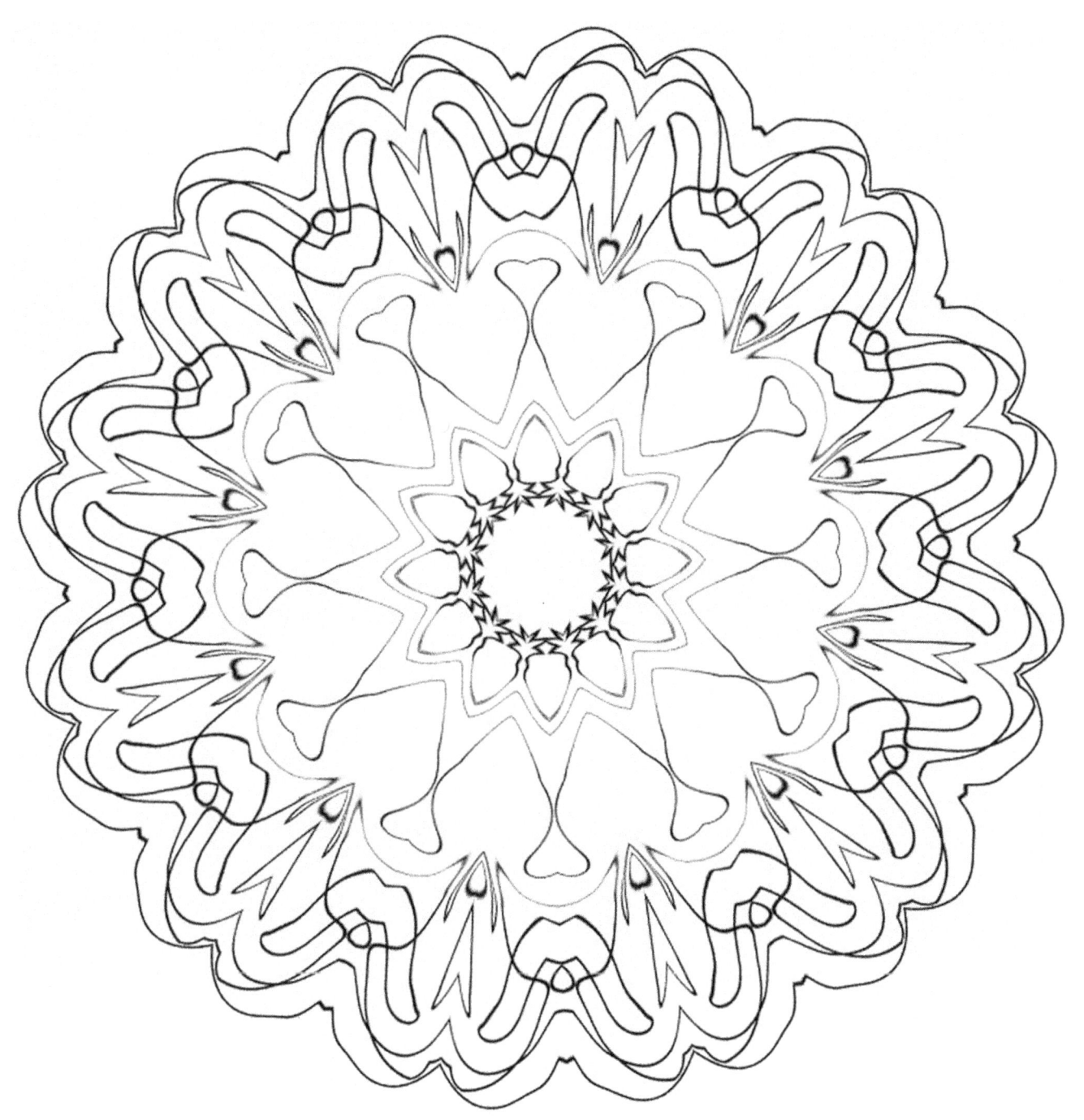

Unite

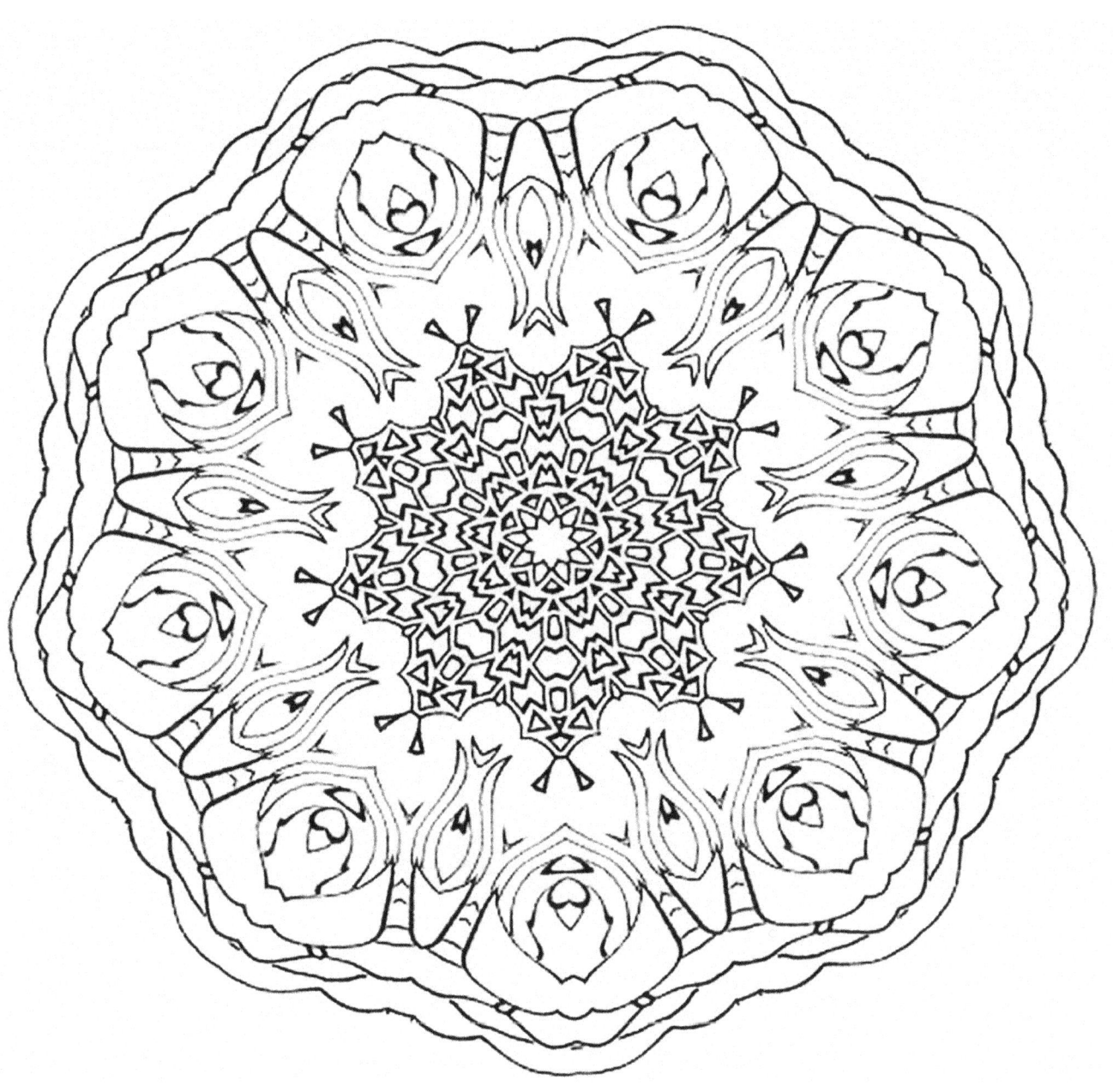

Windmill

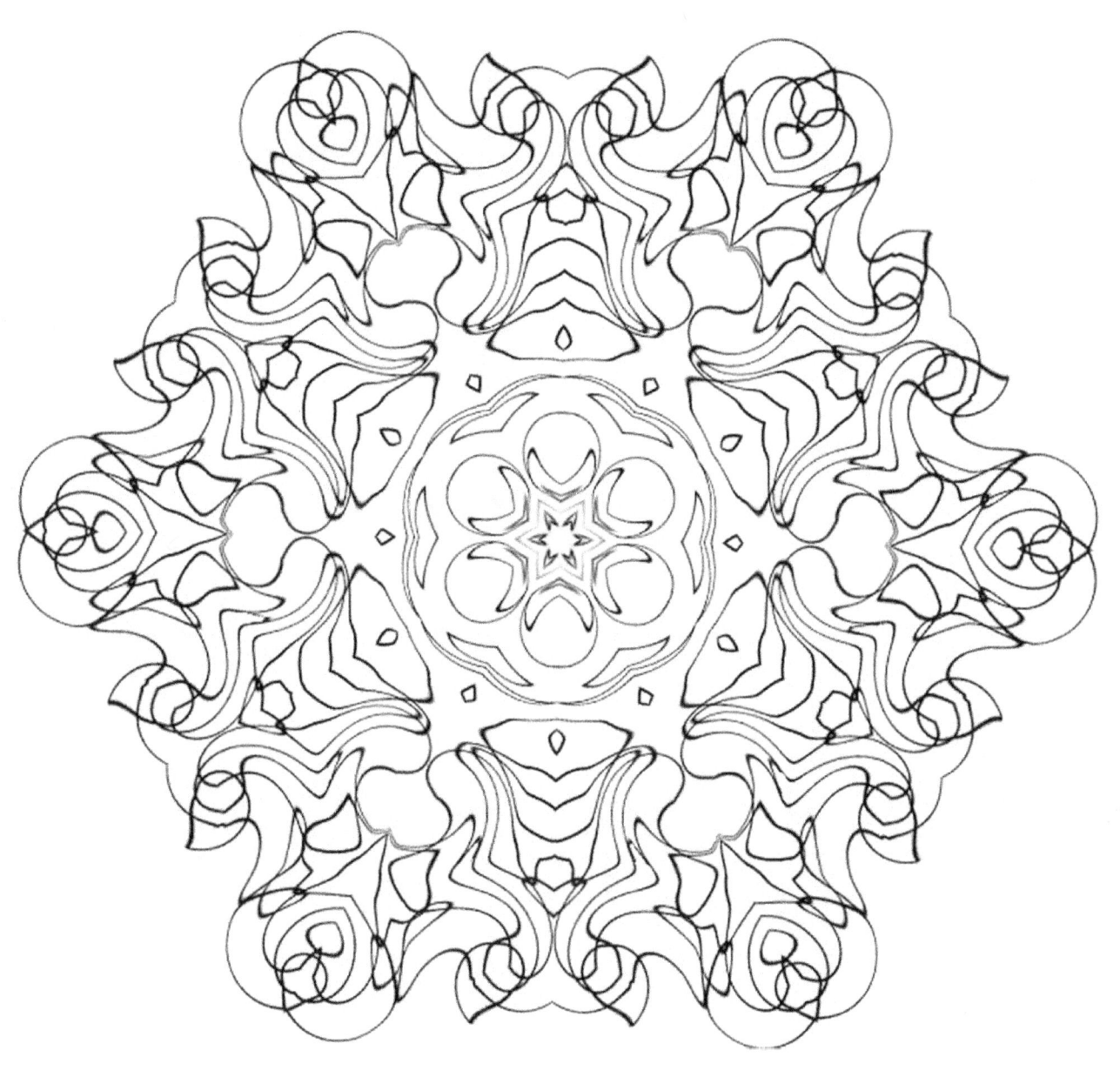

Winged Bells